Sun and Cross

Jakob Streit grew up in Spiez, Switzerland, a district to which Irish monks brought Christianity over a thousand years ago. He studied natural history and history of art. He is a teacher both in child and adult education. For some years he has produced open-air dramatic performances.

Sun and Cross

From megalithic culture
to early Christianity in Ireland

Jakob Streit

Floris Books

Translated by Hugh Latham

First published in German under the title
Sonne und Kreuz
by Verlag Freies Geistesleben, Stuttgart, 1977
First published in English in 1984 by Floris Books
This edition published in 2004 by Floris Books

British Library CIP Data available

ISBN 0-86315-440-9

Printed in Great Britain
By The Bath Press

Contents

III The Spread of Irish Christianity on the Continent

Ireland

Foreword

Accounts of the influence of Irish missionaries in Switzerland and the continent of Europe generally awakened the author's desire to explore old Ireland and old Irish Christianity. Detailed enquiry led as a result to the source, to Ireland herself. In the course of an extensive study of sources the importance of old Ireland for the culture of Northern Europe became more and more evident. Research carried out on journeys through Ireland increased the realization that the megalithic and Celtic culture is the basis and spiritual background on which 'Nordic Christianity' developed. In the last two centuries the picture has become increasingly clear, the picture of a development advancing by stages and transforming itself, changing in a unique manner and developing pre-Christian spirituality into primitive Christianity.

A certain change has become evident in recent years in the interpretation of archaeological discoveries. Instead of merely registering the discovery as fragments and objects of a 'primitive civilization,' in which man is only capable of a 'naive and childish scribble,' a new interpretation has recently been introduced. Leo Probenius endeavoured to construct the bridge leading from prehistory to history, and J.J. Bachofen already in the last century contributed to the recognition of a spiritual continuity.

Marie König in her fundamental work *Am Anfang der Kultur* examines the sign language of early man and defines the task of the archaeologist in these words:

> We must look for an explanation which is based on authentic material discovered but which does not only see facts in a positivist sense in it, but rather an explanation that takes account of the world of the spirit, of the supernatural and transcendental that lies behind the material.[1]

Herbert Kühn remarks in his *Vorgeschichte der Menschheit*: 'In the final analysis it is a question of the man behind the things, who stands behind the rock carvings, of the man who held the pottery bowl in his hands ...'[2] And Marie König asserts: 'The idea that early man was "primitive and stupid" has been left behind.' It is right therefore to bring his mythic-magical experience of the world into archaeological discoveries. The first part of this book seeks to make a contribution in this sense to the study of the megalithic period in old Ireland.

In 1873, in a wide-ranging book on early Christian Ireland (*Die iroschottische Missionskirsche*) the German Protestant theologian J.H. Ebrard attempted to break through to a new view of Irish-Scottish Christianity, a view freed from dogma. The work remained an isolated monument, not least because essential sources were still unknown at that time. A. Bellesheim made a survey from the Catholic point of view in his *Geschichte der katholischen Kirche Irlands*. Then in 1929 in New York there appeared James Kenney's epoch-making collection, *The Sources for the Early History of Ireland* which was later augmented by publications by members of the Irish Archaeological and Celtic Society. Based mainly on Kenney's sources the *Geschichte der irischen Kirche* was published in 1954 by the Berlin Church-historian Walter Delius. Its great service is to have shown that the structure of the old Irish Church was that of an independent, primitive Christian movement of the North that was independent of Rome.

The fine reproductions that are now possible have led to the appearance in recent years of a number of books on old Ireland, which deal in particular with the artistic treasures of Irish Christianity. There is often a danger that only an aesthetic value will be given to this culture.[3]

What it was that came 'from the farthest corner of the world' (which is how Ireland was viewed in the Middle Ages) and so decisively stimulated and humanized the spiritual life of the northern European mainland is insufficiently incorporated in our historical consciousness. This book seeks to contribute to the tracing and rediscovery of Ireland's great spiritual past and to carry the work of Ebrard and Delius further by including material from prehistory.

I

Sun Stones of the Megalithic Culture

1. Megalithic Cult Centres

In this century archaeology has unearthed an abundant quantity of individual discoveries from a great variety of ancient cultures. The description and interpretation of the culture to which the discovery belongs is difficult and requires deep penetration into the forms of life in the period concerned. It was Herbert Spencer (1820–1903) in the nineteenth century who carried Darwin's theory of natural selection of the fittest as an axiom into the field of interpreting early cultures and linked this evolutionary theory to the process of evaluation. As a result the older a culture the more primitive and inferior it was considered. This is the source of the contempt for the 'primitive psyche' of early man and for archaeology contenting itself with cataloguing and dating. The man behind the material aroused no interest. It was not realized that these early human beings had a rich mythic experience of the world and an intimate and close connection with nature. Sagas and folk tales are late witnesses of this.

The quality and volume of a man's spirituality and that of his time is not in proportion to civilizing equipment. World history frequently demonstrates that it is precisely with an increase in civilization that a decline and alienation of spiritual and moral culture can be connected. Consider Ancient Rome, and indeed our own times.

If by culture one understands a creatively active and religious power which later develops by means of cult, custom, symbol and imagery into conceptual thought, one must grant to the men of the primitive culture a wealth of spiritual experience which sustains them in an externally very simple civilization.

> Men of earlier times do not as yet separate their own soul experience from the life of nature. They do not feel that they stand as a special entity beside nature. They experience *themselves* in nature as they experience lightning and thunder in it, the drifting of the clouds, the course of the stars or the growth of plants. What moves man's hand on his own body, what places his foot on the ground and makes him walk, for the prehistoric man, belongs to the same sphere of world forces that also causes lightning, cloud formations and all other external events.[1]

Birth and death, their experience of the sun's influence, the movements of the stars and the weather all spoke powerfully to these primeval people. For them all these were a revelation of creative gods, whose awestruck subject they felt themselves to be. They felt a primal need to raise themselves up towards gods in consecrated places and worship them.

As far back as history can be traced spiritual leaders are found who, as priests, direct this primal religious need. The form and content of their actions varied according to the characteristics of the people. The high cultures of Asia had their religious founders: Krishna, Zoroaster, Buddha. In Hebrew tradition it was the legendary priest Seth who founded the mythical succession of the priesthood, which Aaron later continued. We find Druids and bards among the Northern peoples, and the shamans in northern Asia. The most important of these priesthoods were considered to consist of 'adepts' who by means of trance, transcendental vision or visionary experience established their spiritual ability to guide the clans, the tribes, the peoples. They formed customs and tradition. Comparative research in the twentieth century has revealed an astonishingly similar expression of primal religious elements in all megalithic cultures, which among other things finds expression in stone monuments, in menhirs, dolmens and cromlechs which have a common symbolism.[2] These cultic monuments are so global in their distribution that in order to elucidate the problems of Irish megalithic culture the related stone monuments in Britain and Brittany and in more distant parts of Europe may be considered. Their motifs indicate the same origin and the same tradition.

The menhir*

A stone monument served as a territorial marker in megalithic as well as in later times, when stone markers served as boundary stones to separate plots of land or to indicate state or tribal frontiers; but the erection of an ancient menhir had a spiritual meaning. A magical-religious function adhered to it.[3] Whenever a menhir rises it indicates an earthly centre where the *lower*, earth and man, can link itself with a *higher*, with the cosmos, with the gods. By the menhirs of Er Lannic (Brittany) man-made pits containing burnt pieces of animal bone were found, the remains of ritual fires.[4] The menhir symbolizes mankind striving upwards. J. Röder says of the site of a menhir that it is the place '... where a sacrifice for the gods is carried out and which the divinity accepts.'[5] Such cult centres were often marked also by a stake or (in Northern Europe among the Germans) by a tree.

Rudolf of Fulda (780–865) says of the Germans: 'In the open air they worshipped also a wooden post (*truncus*) of considerable size which they had raised high; in their heathen language they called it *Irminsäule*, which means "pillar of the world" in learned language, just as if it supported the universe.'[6]

The menhirs were 'pillars of the world' of this kind. They marked the place where the priest or priestess joined forces with the gods through the fellowship of the cult. A number of discoveries confirm that ritual fires were lit at the menhirs. It can only be conjectured whether the ritual fire was linked to the mantric word and how far the circuit round the stone had any importance as a type of cultic dance.

* *Men* is Celtic for stone, *hir* means long.

Figure 1. Cromlechs and the menhir of Quiberon.

In Ireland there is a particularly fine menhir at Punchestown (County Kildare). When it was re-erected a burial chamber was found at its base[7] (Figure 2). The cross-section at the base is rectangular and as it rises it becomes the apex of a triangle at a height of 6 to 7 metres (20 to 23 feet). A gentle gradient as it tapers leads upwards with energetic impulse and the form guides the sight to the vault of the sky, to the cosmos.

The graves found at cult centres, menhirs, dolmens and cromlechs tempt to the narrow interpretation that these stone monuments mark out burial places in every case. For megalithic people, no less than in later cultures, the burial places of those who had died were places for communication with the world of the dead, with the world of the spirit. 'No tillage, no marriage and no ceremony of maturity either can take place without contact being established in some way with the dead .... The impression is given that they are the more important part of the community.'[8]

Stonehenge has a broad ring of pits for cremation ashes outside the circle of stones. This shows that the physical remains of cremated bodies were to provide the place for spiritual contact with the dead, with the ancestors. The menhir at Punchestown is a particularly fine and graphic structure expressing this longing and this soaring into the world of the divine, of the cosmos.

The 'sacred centre,' at which the link with the 'above' was solemnized, is the dedicated place where prayers and sacrifices are sent to the gods of the sky. Mircéa Eliade[9] sees in them also the place where priests could ascend into the transcendental world. In the 'centre' communication with and penetration of the world of the divine was sought. In this connection Eliade refers to an ancient ritual of 'ascent.' Early Buddhist texts speak of a 'flight into the sky,' and the *Rig Veda* expresses this request: 'O Tree, see that the sacrifice reaches the gods!' (I.13,11).

From the wealth of traditions referred to by Mircéa Eliade a few can be selected which he summarizes in the following words: 'The power of flight can, as we have seen, be obtained in many ways (shamanic trance, mystical ecstasy, magical techniques), but also by a severe psychological discipline, such as the Yoga of Patañjali ...'[10] Primitive cultures right into Celtic times were able to advance from consciousness deposited in myth an advance which led through trance, vision and ecstasy to a capacity for spiritual experience and perception.

Mantric cult intoning as well as rhythmic singing of words are part of the Celtic rites. In Northern Europe sacred dances and ritual circling had their last adherents as late as the early nineteenth century. C.G. Brunius, whose book about the Swedish rock carvings at Tanum appeared in 1868, experienced as a child in 1818 the dances by the rock carvings derived from the megalithic period. He reported that people had instruments and that they sang and danced and made prescribed gestures. In Brittany barren women visited the menhir, round which they walked and danced. There is a tradition that people used to scrape dust from a menhir at Bassecourt in the Swiss Jura and use it medicinally for earache.[11] In this instance the ancient Druid art of healing has been lost and later attributed to the stone itself.

In France the 'secret cults at the stones' persisted from the fifth to the eighth century and were discussed and attacked at the Council of Arles in 452, of Tours in 577 and of Nantes in 658. In 789 Charlemagne issued an edict against the 'stone worshippers,' which went so far as to threaten them with capital punishment. The fact that in France, above all in Brittany, the stone cult survived so tenaciously into Christian times points to the strength of a culture whose influence can survive for a millennium, a culture whose stone monuments parallel those of Ireland. As some things have survived better in Brittany than in Ireland examples of Breton megaliths are discussed for the purpose of completeness and comparison.

Figure 2. Menhir of Punchestown (County Kildare).

The 'sacred way'

Anyone who visits Carnac and the menhir there with its long lines of stones (the alignments) is struck by the problem of these unusual parallel lines of stones reaching out into the countryside for several hundred metres. We should like to point out two basic characteristics of these monuments, witnesses of an organized cult, monuments which are also found in the Irish menhirs. Two basic types of stones set in the earth are found. The two illustrations show *(a)* the direction downwards from above and *(b)* polarity moving upwards. A wedge is often found placed as a symbol on ritual stones (Figure 5).[12] The downward pointing wedge is both an expression and an image of those forces which descend from the cosmos to influence the earth: the ripening rays of the sun, the lightning flash that fertilizes the earth, the rays of the moon and stars, the falling rain and dew. That is why in ancient Persia, in the spring the king used to strike a golden wedge-shaped dagger into the ploughed earth as a ray of Ohrmazd, and this gave the peasants the signal for sowing the corn.

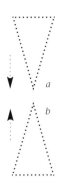

The second shape, that of a pyramid with a broad base which tapers as it rises, gives an answer from below to the impact of the wedges from the cosmos. In prayer, worship and gratitude man raises himself towards the heights. Probably the priests of those Stone Age men who with such strength and effort transported and placed these stones used them to express the two directions of the cosmic cult: one moving downwards from above (the divine action), the other, the human, earthly one pointing upwards in the rite of sacrifice. The stone avenues or alignments consist of both forms alternating.

Figure 3.

Figure 4. Alignments of Carnac.

The layout of these stone avenues has another, a third direction: the horizontal, the direction over the earth; the procession as a sacred line of movement. All the stone avenues we know, with but one or two exceptions, run from east to west, that is to say they follow the path of the sun. Some, that at Kerlescan for example, are fitted to the equinox; others, such as that at Kermario, to the summer solstice. The sevenfold stone alignment at Le Menec begins with very low stones (about 30–40 cm, 12–16 inches). They increase in height as they move towards the west, growing to the height of the human beings in the procession and finally exceeding human height with about 4 metres (13 feet).

In the stone alignments paths of a processional line are clearly discernible, which it is possible to conjecture was combined with singing and rhythmical dancing. Analogy with later examples of 'processional ways' would justify this conjecture.

Figure 5. Ritual Stone of Gavr'inis, Brittany.

west ⟵————————————⟶ east

Figure 6.

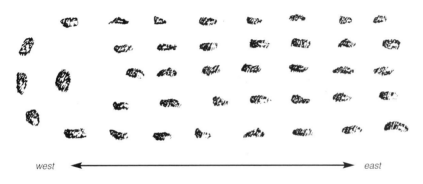

west ⟵————————————⟶ east

Figure 7.

When megalithic man at the Feast of the Sun walked from east to west it meant: 'We are walking along on earth with the path of the sun! We are welcoming the light! As we walk we stay in the light of the sun!' As primitive man at this time worshipped the sun as divine, in their cult they walked along with the sun god and in his path. As a result of this procession in the light the force linking them with the divine increased, and this was demonstrated by the increase in the height, the 'growth' of the stone. At the end of the alignments the stones stand in a semicircle. One lower central stone marks the place, it is conjectured, where the sacrifice was solemnized as the climax of the cult of the sun.

A careful examination of the angle of the alignments gave the bearings seen overleaf in relation to sunrise in the case of the three most important avenues at Carnac:[13]

Kerlescan

Position of sunrise east-west at equinox

Le Ménec

Position of sunrise early May/early August connected with ripening corn (opposite sunset in early November/early February)

Kermario

Position of sunrise at midsummer (opposite sunset at midwinter)

W ◄- - - - - - - - - - - -╆- - - March 21
                                   Sept 23

May 6
Aug 8
W
         E

(Nov 8)
(Feb 4)

June 21
W
     E
(Dec 21)

This investigation of the angles confirms that the stone avenues were places where men in those days could share the experience of the sun's year. In this way the cult effected the link with the high gods of light, above all with the sun god, with the 'Light of the World.' The cult of the sun must have been the most important cult of megalithic man.

Stone avenues are known in Ireland too, although as Ó Ríordáin remarks, it is these stones that for the most part have been carried off as building material.[14] The modest avenues at Castlenalact (County Cork), Beenalaght (County Cork), Shantemon (County Cavan) have survived. Sometimes avenues can be found linked with stone circles, so that the 'procession' advances into a cromlech, the straight line (path) and circle (altar, sacrifice) producing a powerful effect which certainly played an important part in the cult (Figure 8).

A long time must be spent growing familiar with the stone monuments of that countryside before it is possible to become sensitive to the language of their forms. When we study and gaze at those weathered forms, walk again and again through those lines of stones the impression grows on us which Werner Schüpbach has aptly described:

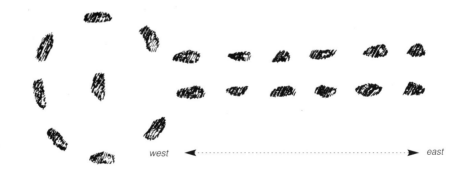

west ◄- -► east

Figure 8.

A feeling of infinite isolation and loneliness overcomes us in these places. The air seems to us to be thin, empty and silent .... But then the greatness and the customs of a distant, forgotten time begin to speak. In the cromlechs and avenues we can trace as though in a skeleton the hieroglyphs of a life that once had meaning and significance.[15]

In these places men joined together to carry out their great cult rituals in honour of nature and the gods, joined together under the leadership of their priests for the influence of the creative world spirit on the earth and in the cosmos.

Stone circles and cromlechs*

The literature of prehistory lists about two hundred stone circles (cromlechs) still surviving today in Ireland and Britain. If the menhir indicates the 'sacred centre' which informs man of the link between earth and heaven, the avenue, the 'sacred way,' leads to the place of sacrifice, where the ritual is consummated. In the cromlech we find a special circular area marked out. Stonehenge in southern England is a famous example. It has fascinated archaeologists since the eighteenth century. The work of excavation by R.J.C. Atkinson and the bold calculations by the astronomer G.S. Hawkins have proved that this important cromlech was aligned in a complicated fashion with the positions of moon and sun in such a way that the position of the stones could be used to foretell eclipses of the moon. On the other hand all the other bearings of the stones were tested by a computer but revealed no connection with the planets.

It is generally recognized that the cromlechs had no utilitarian importance; their importance in the life of men living in myth was in cultic ritual. They were also a part of the priesthood's task of bringing human life in the passage of the year into harmony with the year's cosmic order. Obviously this found expression above all in the rhythms of sun and moon.

Simple cromlechs with low stones were to be found in great numbers. Very often the tumuli (burial mounds) were surrounded by cromlechs (Newgrange and other sites). The circular form gave the stone circle the character of a symbol of the cosmos (zodiac). The small cromlechs certainly did not assist any astronomical calculation; their function was simply to demarcate a 'sacred place.'

The circle of stones round the hills of Newgrange and Knowth have symbols carved on them. These mostly point to the sun as the mystery of all life, as will be explained in a later chapter. The stress on the centre is as part of the circle of the cosmos. From this point it is sustained and radiation beamed. At Stonehenge the central altar is set slightly away from the centre, and as a result the priest

* *Crom* is Celtic for curved, round; *lech* means place.

stood in the exact centre as he performed the ceremony. We found a particularly striking central stone at the Breton tumulus of Kermario at Carnac, which rises from the centre of the tumulus while the cromlech forms a loose circle a little outside the tumulus. Unfortunately a fine site at Quibéron with an exceptionally tall central stone no longer exists. A drawing of it made in the nineteenth century is preserved (Figure 1).[16]

The *Dinn-senchus* is a collection of Irish sagas, which are linked with place names, the oldest going back to the eleventh century. It is stated that on the plain of Magh Slecht (County Cavan) a cromlech was laid out. Crom Crúaich, with a central stone adorned with gold and silver, and that round the central stone were twelve stones decorated with copper figures. With the gold-silver of the centre (sun-moon) and round it in a circle the twelve divisions of the zodiac, this site could be regarded as the 'ideal cromlech.'[17]

For mythic man the cosmos (circle) is spiritually and creatively centred by the (masculine) sun. In the centre connection to the 'light of the world' is established. We can imagine the officiating priest in the centre of the cromlech where the altar stone stands, and around the circle of stones the assembled tribe receiving the radiation of the 'rays emitted by the centre.' It is here that the circular procession (circumambulation of the centre), a well known part of ancient cults, may have originated. In contrast to the rectilinear-earthly procession the circular motion in cult ritual manifested the rudiments of cosmic motion. Here were the origins of the 'round dance,' the sacred dance in a circle. (According to Charpentier the Gaelic name for Stonehenge was Cathoir Gall, which can be roughly translated as 'Hall of the Giants' Dance.'[18] A parallel can be found in the Greek mysteries. Lucian, a Greek writer of the second century, says quite plainly: 'Not a single ancient religious rite can be found without dancing ...' For Ireland there are only stones, no written tradition from that legendary time. This is also true of Brittany.

All the stone emplacements we have described are pre-Celtic monuments. Stonehenge has been placed in the seventeenth century BC.[19] By analogy the corresponding Irish sites can be placed at the turn of the second and third millenia BC.[20]

Diodorus Siculus (first century BC) has an interesting passage about cromlechs in general and Stonehenge in particular. He writes about a sun cult in a northern island.

> This island lies close to the North Pole. It is inhabited by Hyperboreans ... There are stories that Apollo is honoured there above all other gods. On this island there is also a magnificent temple precinct consecrated to the sun god and ... a temple of the God which is circular ...[21]

Figure 9. Stone circle at Dunbeacon (County Cork).

Summing up, we may assume that among the peoples of Northern Europe in pre-Christian times there were cultures characterized throughout by religious cults, and information about them is given us by the dumb, silent witnesses of stone. This is particularly true of Ireland's lonely countryside. They were devoted to linking man with the cosmos, human life with the influence of the gods. Here arose not only the dates and the forms of ritual for the yearly celebrations, but also instructions for sowing, for harvest and other rustic activities, which have survived as a decadent memory in peasant custom and rules. By the cult and its continuation in custom the individual human being became a member of a living community of earth and cosmos. He became part of the universal circle, of the universal cromlech. Goethe expressed this poetically:

> According to eternal and unbreakable laws
> We must all complete the circle of our being ...[22]

The 'Priests of the Stone' tried on the level of nature religion to convey this to men whose life and perception had been prepared for reverence.

Dolmens, graves, cults of the dead

Human graves and human bones or ashes have been found at almost all the sites of cult stones. This has often tempted archaeologists to see only grave stones in the dolmen and menhirs. In Ireland in the megalithic period the dead were often cremated. Cults of the dead at first had the purpose of sustaining and cultivating community with the dead. They also had the aim of placating the *mana* of the dead man, of bringing him a peaceful 'rest.' The place where the dead man or his ashes rested was consecrated ground. The dolmen, stones standing upright with a stone

Figure 10. Dolmen.

roof laid over them, is in Western Europe above all an early form of building over a grave. The dolmen could also serve as a 'place for meditation' or be used as a sacrificial altar (Figure 10).

In Wales the dolmens are called Druids' altars. In ancient times the function of a burial monument was commonly linked with more far-reaching uses than providing a memorial of the dead. Free-standing dolmen are known which were not burial places.[23] 'Leac an Scáil' is the name of the dolmen at Kilmogue. Translated this means: 'The stone which throws a shadow.' This indicates that the Druids could get some information from the light and shade thrown by the stones in the course of the day.

After studying the dolmens and cromlechs of Wales Rudolf Steiner summarized his impressions as follows:

> When we look at the single dolmens we find that they are really instruments whereby the outer physical effects of the Sun were shut off in order that the Initiate who was gifted with seership could observe the effects of the Sun in the dark space. The inner qualities of the Sun element, how these permeate

the Earth, and how they are again radiated back from the Earth into cosmic space — this was what the Druid priest was able to observe in the single cromlechs [dolmens]. The physical nature of the light of the Sun was warded off, a dark space was created by means of the stones, which were fitted into the soil with a roof stone above them and in this dark space it was possible by the power of seeing through the stones to observe the spiritual nature and being of the Sun's light.[24]

Rudolf Steiner regarded the dolmens as places where intuitive knowledge of the activity of light had been made possible for a spiritually trained priest. In the cromlechs on the other hand he saw equipment which already gave the pre-Celtic Druid a vital relationship with the sun calendar of the year, which he used as a basis for his decisions on sowing, harvest and so on.

The 'cults of the graves and the dead' raise the question of what ideas of immortality were held in those times. In detailed studies Hans Hartmann has described the survival into modern times in Ireland of pre-Christian burial rites.[25] In the west of the island there were still at the beginning of the twentieth century districts where no priest of the Church would dare to conduct a burial service. This was carried out by the people themselves according to ancient tradition. After an unusual and frequently boisterous wake the dead body was carried three times round the house. Mourning women in front and behind the coffin expressed their grief in loud melodious cries. The procession with the corpse had to circle once round the cemetery sunwise. Care of the grave is neglected in these districts out of fear of the dead man's 'mana.' Most of the cemeteries in the countryside of Western Ireland are a long way from the villages and to this day are covered by grass and desolate. On the other hand old people under the spell of primitive ideas often visit the graves of children, as they hope that this will bring an early return for themselves after death.

The idea of rebirth (reincarnation) was familiar to the ancient Celtic world. Caesar reported the Druids 'teach that souls do not die but after death pass into other bodies ....' G. Dottin[26] takes up this idea and enlarges it. 'The idea they [the Druids] particularly advocated was that the soul does not die but passes after death into another body *after a cycle of years.*'[27] The widely-travelled Greek historian Diodorus Siculus mentions that Celts at cremation ceremonies threw letters (parchment) into the fire, in order to convey information to their dead in the other world.[28]

Even today when someone dies in Ireland the expression is used 'he sailed' or 'he had a good crossing.' And the crossing refers to the setting of the sun in the west, which opens the way into the cosmos of the night, into the realm of the dead. For mythic humankind the dead were invisible people living among them.

For dead men of importance special dolmens were erected and as a result of being covered with further gifts of stone they became tumuli. 'There are graves of important persons of prehistoric times which are still being honoured with gifts of stone today.[29] Dolmens which are arched over and covered by stones are also called cairns. They are often as high as a house. By means of gifts of stone over a lengthy period of time they have grown to their present-day height of stone hills. This is a pleasant thought, particularly compared with the pyramid graves of Egypt, which were built by the forced labour of slaves. The inhabitants of Balingarry, for instance, have told of this building of cairns.[30]

If prehistoric humankind sought a path to the gods of the cosmos through menhirs, dolmens, cromlechs and stone avenues, the tumulus (the cave) provided the inner connection to the earth, to the world of the dead, to themselves. Recesses and stone shelves in the interior of tumuli show that a man (a priest?) could enter at all times through an entrance that was kept open. Here he had a quiet place, completely shut off from the outside world and suitable for contemplation and meditation. The stone carvings in the interior of the cairn, mostly of sun themes, indicate the search for the inner Sun, the inner Light. In the next chapter a tumulus of this kind and its symbols will be described. But first of all a fundamental understanding of the nature of mythic symbolism is necessary.

2. The Sun in Pre-Christian Signs and Symbols

The idea of a symbol

Among the oldest records of spiritual history are symbolic signs which are either figurative or entirely geometric. In all ancient cultures they precede picture signs, as they do word or letter signs. They made certain conclusions possible concerning prehistoric religious ideas. In the era of myth a symbol acquired cultic-magical significance. Meditative absorption in its structure and background was to link mythic man more closely with a supersensory, transcendent, spiritual reality. A symbol acquired the task of linking the world of the senses with the world of the spirit.

The word *symbolon* had the meaning for the ancient Greeks 'to join what is separated, to join together.' Many peoples have had a custom that a messenger had to show a broken-off piece of a ring or tablet or stone which could be fitted to the missing part to restore a complete whole. In an extended sense the symbol can be said to contribute the half part to an 'earthly mystery.' This half part is a supersensory completion which joins together again the unity which had been broken in two. This has been a profound concern of all religions, which have used the symbol as a means of or key to reunification. In some mysteries the ordained priest revealed his identity on entering the temple by means of a verbal symbol (a secret word).

Symbols are one of the most essential components of every occult religious practice. But in ancient times the symbol was never merely an intellectual, conceptual allusion, an external sign that had a definite, understandable meaning. The symbol had to lead to spiritual perception, to develop spiritual experience by means of which man was able to 'climb down' to the powers of the lower world. It was expected that immersion in meditation would develop a soul that, taught and influenced by the symbol and the experiences linked with it, would acquire the ability to perceive supersensory reality. Preparation and training of this sort was practised in the initiation for the priesthood. The trained priest was then received into the circle of those who controlled the practice of cult and symbol. In this symbolism, each individual would give the same symbolic sign a deeper interpretation as he advanced step by step in the maturity of his understanding. For the instinctive understanding of the people it was enough that they worship the symbol as an emblem of something lofty and divine. The priesthood kept the esoteric meaning and its use in meditation as its own mystery.

The runes, which later were reduced to mere letters of an alphabet, were

Teutonic religious symbols. The saying that Odin 'hung on a tree' for nine days and nights to acquire the wisdom of the runes refers to the rite of initiation. 'Tree' in Teutonic nature symbolism is the sign of the bond between 'heaven and earth.' The branches of the tree-top receive emanations from the cosmos which communicate with the roots through the trunk. An early Indian text of the *Rig Veda* (I.13.14) prays: 'O tree, at this sacrifice reach the gods!'

A noteworthy discovery resulting from research into prehistoric symbols is that the basic symbols display an astonishing similarity in all the widely differing continents of the earth, the symbol of the sun, for instance. Migration has been abandoned as an inadequate explanation of such global universality. On the other hand there is an inclination to accept the view that similar inner experience by men in different epochs and in different parts of the earth lead independently of each other to similar symbols. In this view the resemblance should be traced back to a similar experience of the inner spiritual content of the same force, of which the symbol is the outer, demonstrative sign.

In the following section an attempt is made to get closer to the remaining traces of megalithic nature and sun worship by unravelling the symbols on a stone covered with symbolic signs, part of an Irish cairn (tumulus). While doing so it must be borne in mind that symbols can have several meanings. A circle, for instance, with a centre can mean 'sun' and at the same time 'man and universe,' or the central point and circumference of a cult centre. Symbols, therefore, should not be defined too rigidly, but interpreted according to the place where they are found and its cultic connections.

The central stone in the tumulus of Slieve na Caillighe

North-west of Dublin, near Oldcastle in County Meath, are the Loughcrew Hills. On their heights, in a lonely stretch of country a few square miles in area a number of tumuli, stone circles and standing stones stand out, and their layout gives the impression of an extensive sacral region. From the hilltops there is a view over green plains to the distant mountains. A free region of unspoilt nature spreads out all round. There is a climb up to the completely open tumulus on Slieve na Caillighe. On the hilltop, which is about 275 metres (900 feet) in height, men of the Stone Age piled up an artificial pyramid-shaped hillock, using tens of thousands of unworked stones, which they carried up the hill to vault over the sacred place on the hilltop. Round Loughcrew a large number of graves has been found. An explanation has already been given of how these were drawn into a cult in prehistoric times. By means of the dead the earth was consecrated as a place for encounter with the supersensory world.

An unusual stone block on the slope of the pyramid forms a powerful, freestanding altar stone with two 'horns.' Its oustanding position points clearly to its ritual function. A large number of participants could assemble in front of it and have a clear view of what took place on the altar stone.

Figure 11. Altar stone with two 'horns.'

Figure 12 (below). Slieve na Caillighe.

The entrance

Standing on the highest point of these hills it is possible to walk towards the narrow entrance of this tumulus. The passage is bordered by shored-up blocks of stone and the ground plan is in the form of an extended cross.

If a place like this is visited with merely superficial interest nothing will be experienced of the feelings of unison which were brought to such a sacred place, especially holy because of its lofty position. It was part of an awed experience of the world by men of the Stone Age. 'To go into the cave' also meant in myth 'to go into the earth,' where the dead are resting: a path into the mystery of inwardness, of silence, of secrecy. If a man stood in the open on the hilltop in the rays of the warmth-bringing, fruit-bearing sun, which shines all round on thousands of its creatures, on trees, flowers and animals, that man would be overcome and

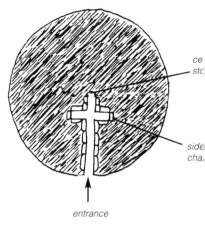

ce
stc

side
cha.

entrance

Figure 13. Plan and entrance to the tumulus of Slieve na Caillighe.

surrender himself in worship to this inexhaustible source of light. He knew that no eye might with impunity stare into its rays and that no hand could ever touch its fire. Its departure brought natural man darkness, fear, and loss. In the night the glittering stars reassured him that the light penetrates all darkness. The sunrise in the morning, its returning strength after the winter solstice, strengthened the conviction that light and life were always victorious in the battle against darkness and death, and that as a result all creatures on earth and man also stay in the light.

The sun symbols belong to the oldest of all symbols that men have carved on stones, rocks and bones. Their god was not our physical sun. The sun for them was the eye and the raiment of the divine, was a revelation of the highest principle of the earth and mankind and the cosmos, a visibly-creating being which revealed itself to men in mythical form as an all-embracing essence of light. The ancient Indians called it Deva, the shining one, the Persians Ahura Mazda, the Egyptians Osiris, the Greeks Apollo, the Celts Lug, the Teutons Balder. They were all the godhead working and operating behind and through the light.

Placed in this overwhelming light mythic man saw himself as a 'Child of the Sun.' This was the central theme of all the ancient religions. In Ireland the cult of the sun lived on to the threshold of the new age. Thus in Galway at the turn of the century the women taking part in the ceremony still walked twelve times round the sun fire which had been lit.[1] The old Irish maypole had a ring with a golden ball in its centre. People used to dance round it in a circle. Fire served as the earthly representative of the sun, as its earthly brother. According to tradition the Druids used to light a fire in a ritual centre at Beltane on the first of May as they completed the sacrifice. The 'seed' of this fire was carried to surrounding districts by relays of runners.[2] Such customs and 'ideas of light' lived in the feelings of those people who carried their stones up to Slieve na Caillighe and it is not surprising to meet a row of sun symbols in the interior.

The central stone

It is something more than a beautiful experience to walk in chambers like this by candlelight. The living flame in a breath of air brings an inner room like this to life quite differently from the way the harsh light of an electric bulb does. Suddenly we are standing at the intersection of the corridor. To right and left are small side chambers, marked off by stone slabs. One chamber is half closed. A man could find space to sit in it. The main recess at the end of the corridor terminates with a central stone (Figure 14), which has on it a number of unusual symbols. They have been cut deep into the stone. With almost magical force the mystery surrounding them at first prevents examination. Signs are found here on this central stone which otherwise can only be found scattered over a number of sites. Let us try to draw on the comparative study of symbols and elucidate the meaning of these signs.

Figure 14. The central stone in the tumulus of Slieve na Caillighe.

Figure 15.

The sun motif

The sun is the main theme of these symbols engraved in stone. Eleven consist of a circle with a centre. Three of these are a circle in its most basic form with an accentuated centre, which is still used today in astronomical calendars as the sign for the sun. Then there is the sun as a circle with irregular rays radiating and an accentuated centre.

In place of rays leaves resembling flowers also appear in varying numbers, surrounded by an outer circle. Finally there is a fourth variation which has the sun image in the centre with leaves arranged in the shape of the cross, a remarkable anticipation of the later Irish Christian sun cross.

Unmistakably these symbols in the tumulus demonstrate the worship of the light of the world which we have described. But why precisely here inside the dark cave are there these images of the light? The 'cave' was for mythic man a place for spiritual introspection, a place for inner reality, for initiation. The cave had an important place in the rites of initiation in archaic cultures. North American shamans explained '... it is in caves that aspirants [neophytes] have their dreams and meet their helping spirits.'[3] Did these symbols in the innermost part of the cairn assist immersion in meditation? In the side chambers the images are strangely engraved in the roofing stone above the chamber. In order to see them one has to crouch, almost lie, in the chamber, which suggests that this was the position usually adopted in connection with them.

Outside by the tumulus there is a cromlech (sun stone circle) in the light of the day. As we have already seen, this sets man in the sun year, in the cosmos. Inside, in the 'cave,' in the darkness the light is sought as an inner experience. The manner in which this was carried out remains a mystery.

How stubbornly pre-Christian sun rituals have survived in Ireland is shown by the fact that in certain districts right up until the twentieth century only water that the sun has shone was fit for drinking. Nocturnal water was taboo. Burning torches representing the sun were dipped in water to improve lakes and springs.[4]

Throughout Europe prehistoric sun symbolism can be found as far back as Ancient Egypt, where the hieroglyph for the sun god Ra was also a circle with a centre. H.R. Engler[6] summarizes his wide-ranging investigation of sun symbolism thus:

> We arrive at the conclusion that megalithic culture was very widespread over our globe, ranging from Easter Island in the Pacific as far as India. The symbols for the sun were everywhere the same, only the way in which they were combined and their style show any variation.[5]

The symbol of the sun is also identical with the form in the oldest European cult centres. Thus the arrow or the tree in the middle of a round, enclosed site appears among all the Teutonic peoples. In Iceland heaps of stones are found in a circular enclosure, among the Alemannians the oak tree or lime tree was the sacred centre.

The comb motif

On the circumference of the eight-leaved 'sun-flower' are two shapes like a comb. This comb motif occurs world-wide. Hottentots in Southern Africa draw the comb shape when asked to draw rain.[6] Herbert Kühn[7] reports from California and Nevada that an Indian woman called this comb shape a 'cloud with rain.' On prehistoric water jars this comb shape is frequently found. How such symbols persist is shown by a Peasants' Calendar of Graz,[8] which still prints the comb shape like this:

Figure 16.

The centre stone of our tumulus displays the comb shape twice on the outer 'sky circle,' drawn round the flower-like sun symbols. Rain as 'heaven's water' is another primal element, which megalithic man greatly reverenced. It is right that its symbol should be on the 'sacred stone.'

The zig-zag motif

Closely connected with the rain motif is the fourfold zigzag motif on top of the central stone. In the symbolism of children's drawings a zigzag line is commonly used for lightning. Herbert Kühn[10] reports from New Mexico that he saw Indian women painting very old traditional images on their pottery: 'A zigzag line occurs frequently. I asked in Spanish what it meant. The woman said, "That is lightning, and when there is lightning, then the rain comes, and rain is good."'

In this statement lightning, rain and water are linked with each other. In it we can see a pointer to the zigzag images of other ancient cultures.

Egyptian hieroglyph	∧∧∧	= *nu*	= water
Chinese sign	∧∧∧	= *shui*	= water
Semitic letter	∧∧	= *mem*	= water

For people living in myth, lightning and rain were cosmic events brought about by the gods. 'The lightning is also a ray of light, which appears in the sky, and it is also a symbol of the divine light which can indeed bring destruction ... [but] which releases the waters of the sky, which fertilize the earth.'[10] In this sense it is right that 'lightning and rain' should be on the sacred stone, and this verifies a passage in the Glossary of Carnac[11] which reports that the custom was observed in pre-Christian Ireland of placing images of the elements and of the sun on the stone altars. Thus in Fourknocks (County Meath) there is an altar stone whose longest side is entirely covered with fourfold zigzags.[12]

The ladder motif

Figure 17.

This occurs twice on the central stone, once as an image with seven steps which are enclosed; on its right are eight steps, with the enclosing sphere broken open, and a top and bottom curve outlined.

Whenever the motif of the ladder, the steps and gradation appears in the context of a religious cult it refers to the ascending path of an initiate. It concerns the steps to climb to a higher maturity, to a higher consciousness. The ladder rises from the earthly and material to spiritual experience.

In the Egyptian *Book of the Dead* these words are found: 'The gods made a ladder for him so that with its help he might climb to heaven.' In the Old Testament Jacob in his flight experienced contact with the supersensory in the vision of the ladder, the ladder to heaven. The ladder is identical with the 'Tree of Life' which the shaman priest climbed during the ritual, seeking connection with the divine. 'The Altaic shaman climbs a sacred tree or post notched with seven ... tapty' which correspond to the seven planets. When there were eight notches, the last referred to the fixed stars.[13]

It is reasonable to interpret the ladders with seven and with eight steps on the central stone in this way, especially as close to the 'ladders' on their left, is what could be a representation of a man that is like a pentagram.

The bowl motif

From the (microcosmic) viewpoint of human beings 'the bowl' is the motif of an attitude of acceptance, of receiving. It is the attitude of *homo religiosus*, a readiness to become a spiritual receptacle. It is the prerequisite of spiritual quest, of prayer, of the ability to receive revelation. On the central stone the bowl motif is rightly placed at the bottom, ready to receive the abundant revelation released by the images above it.

In the mythic experience of the macrocosm the moon represents the motif of the bowl. The moon-bowls that empty and replenish themselves rhythmically in the phases of the moon reveal reception followed by surrender of the sun's light. On the outer side on the right the bowl motif is found a second time. Here it is completed by four downward lines, which demonstrate the filling of the bowl.

Synopsis of symbols

A synopsis of symbols on the central stone reveals outlines of a cosmic-religious consciousness, which was already serving the pre-Celtic inhabitants of Ireland. It was guided by a priestly tradition which has left only aphoristic images of its activity. Titus Burckhardt's formulation can be applied here:

> For an archaic culture, one that is really still close to nature, every form, however abstract it may be, has a matter of course a purpose and a name ... and for that reason there is no actual representation of nature but only images which express the cosmic event in its entirety and with a regard to its eternal foundation.

The rune stone on Loughcrew with its symbols gives an impressive picture of megalithic awe in face of the cosmos-earth-man experience.

Sun symbols in Newgrange

The mound at Newgrange (County Meath) in the valley of the Boyne was a neolithic sacred place with a burial ground. It is the largest tumulus in Ireland (diameter 80 metres, 265 feet, height 13 metres, 45 feet). The surface is said to have been covered originally with stones of white quartz which have recently been restored. This would have enabled the hill to be a knoll of light in daytime, pointing out a sacred place, whose rays could be seen from far off in the flat countryside. In fine weather Newgrange can be seen from as far away as Tara, the ancient seat of the high kings of Ireland.

A gigantic circle of stones surrounded the mound with more than thirty tall, erect blocks. Only part of this still exists today. The circular base of the hillock itself was

Figure 18. Tumulus of Newgrange.

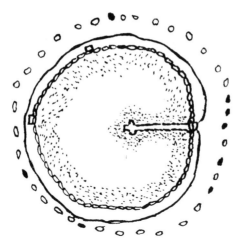

Figure 19. Plan of Newgrange.

lined with long stones laid flat, some of which display motifs chiselled with superb technique. At the entrance the most complete spiral stone in all Ireland is found (Figure 20).

Apart from the spirals, the main motifs at Newgrange are the zigzag line already discussed and the concentric sun motif. The rhomboid and lozenge appear particularly frequently. We shall now examine the question of why the lozenge* should also be a sun motif.

The double spiral gives the sun's dynamic in a year. Proceeding from the centre (winter) the unfolding and developing half is to be identified with the growth of the sun's power as far as summer. The second half, reducing and waning, goes by way of autumn as far as winter.

---

* In what follows the term 'rhomboid' is used.   *Figure 21 (opposite). Spirals.*

Figure 20. The spiral stone at the entrance of Newgrange.

The combination of symbols on one of the long surrounding stones is of interest (Figure 23).

The 'summer sun' can be seen as a rhomboid in the centre above the double spiral, where the left half of the year has fully unrolled from the winter point to the summer solstice (June 21). Moving to the right the spiral revolves into the winter half of the year as far as the winter point. Underneath the double spiral the 'lower sun' appears, the winter sun represented and so to speak 'imprisoned' by a double rhomboid.

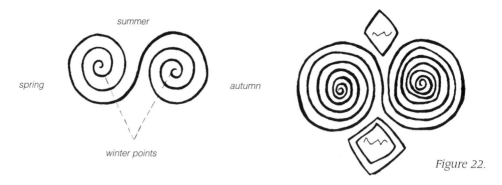

Figure 22.

Figure 23. Stone from the circle around the tumulus of Newgrange.

Figure 24. Chain of rhomboids at Newgrange.

In the interior of the tumulus rhomboids are found arranged together in free sequence. One outer long stone has the same motif series, but in strict geometrical sequence, in which the vertical diagonal of each rhomboid is drawn. The chain of rhomboids suggests the idea of a representation of the cycle of the year. If we follow the plane of rhomboid as it increases and then decreases again we realize we are following the sun year's rhythm of growth and diminution, as it is also represented by the spiral. Here a rhomboid represents a sun year (Figure 24).

What is expressed by dynamic movement in the preceding double spiral image is also realized in the plane of the rhomboid. The vertical diagonal shows the longest day as the middle of the sun year. The chain of joined rhomboids is the symbolic image of the ongoing chain of sun years. Rhomboid and spiral can both be recognized as *dynamic* sun symbols, just as the circle with a centre is a *static* sun image.

When an elderly guide at Newgrange (he had been a guide there for over fifty years) conducted the author round the tumulus in 1966 he pointed out a rhomboid engraved on the stone in the interior. He explained that he had noticed that every year at the time of the shortest days in December a ray of the sun came through the long and narrow entrance after sunrise and fell exactly on this spot. This showed that the sun in one of its most important positions, the winter solstice, was pointed out by the

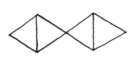
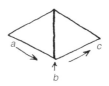
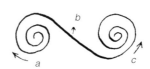

Figure 25.

rhomboid. The passage collapsed during restoration work, and unfortunately the original phenomenon can no longer be observed, as the entrance has been altered.

The sun rhomboid has been found on many prehistoric sites. For Southern England R.J.C. Atkinson describes the grave of a warrior whose sun emblem with its threefold circle lay above his head and on whose breast a metal, threefold rhomboid image was found.[14] It was taken for granted by many peoples who practised the cult of the sun that a warrior should fight under the sign of the sun, of the light.

The two sun symbols are beautifully combined on a grave bowl motif of the Hallstatt period in the Museum zu Allerheiligen in Schaffhausen, Switzerland.

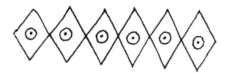

Figure 26.

In the northern chamber of Newgrange we find a roof stone with an engraving embossed. In the centre is the sun year (rhomboid) surrounded by eight circles, which represent perhaps the eight stages of the sun in the course of the year; they are so positioned that a second, outer rhomboid can be discerned.

The central stone of the tumulus at Fourknocks (County Meath) has an interesting combination of sun-rhomboid and moon-bowl motifs.[15]

Figure 27.

Fascinating in the range of its images is an outer stone with very clear textures and marks of drilling, demonstrating a consciously organizing will to design creatively (Figures 28 and 29).

There is a remarkable bisection. A vertical, dividing panel runs down the middle of the stone. On the left at the top of the left half are reverse spirals, the path of life and death (see pp. 53f). Referring to the sun, the reverse spiral signifies the halves of the sun year, the unfolding and also the subsequent diminishing. Underneath are panels of rhomboids arranged in sequence, signifying the chain of years succeeding each other. On the right of the dividing panel is found one of the puzzling image forms at Newgrange whose meaning we might try to

Figures 28 (above) and 29 (detail). Stone from the circle around the tumulus of Newgrange.

find in one or two primary elements. It appears to be a type of stone panel with shapes similar to those found on other flanking stones which possibly had basic meaning for the priests in their role of educators and instructors. Otherwise they would hardly have been carved in stone. It is clear that these shapes had no decorative purpose, and one realizes this if one allows these deliberately shaped, undecorative forms to exert their influence.

Both basic motifs show wedges with lines enclosing them. One wedge points downwards from above: sun (light) is emerging from the cosmos *(a)*; another wedge points up from below: earth (human) is raising itself up towards the cosmos *(b)*.

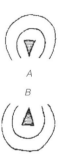

A

B

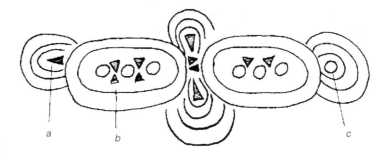

Figure 30

Like a seed in its pod, the wedge is here in a realm of forces marked out by lines. Both types are found in great numbers, but that with the wedge pointing downwards predominates. In addition there is a series of wedges pointing horizontally from right to left. This is of course the direction of the sun from east to west. A few wedges point from left to right (west to east), that is to say in the direction of the rising run.

The central motif uniquely displays all four cosmic directions:

a: Sun declining westward (?)

b: Three drilled holes and wedges facing up and down

c: Sun symbol, full strength in the east (?)

The stone has some holes drilled which have no connection with basic engraved shapes. They seem to have been drilled here and there quite unsystematically. Do they perhaps belong to a later time, when the meaning of these images was no longer known or respected?

Because of its symbols Newgrange ranks as one of the most important centres of a prehistoric sun cult. Its structure goes far beyond the requirements of an outstanding burial ground.

The sun stone at Tully

This stone at Tully (County Dublin) throws additional light on the sun motifs of pre-Christian Ireland (Figure 31). It shows a three-tiered sun on a stone which widens towards the top. The three suns are joined by a vertical bar from which emanate crenations resembling rays. In the surrounding district there are other examples of these remarkable slabs which have similar motifs. They are known as the Rathdown Slabs. In Figure 31 the conic form, narrowing towards the bottom, represents the cosmic 'arrowhead of light.' The vertical bar could be understood as 'the sun's path,' and the lowest, smallest sun as the winter sun, the middle one above as the sun of the equinox, and the highest and largest as the summer sun.

Figure 31. Stone of Tully, Cabinteely (County Dublin)

Motifs at Knowth

In the neighbourhood of Newgrange is the great tumulus at Knowth, where excavation and investigations have been going on for some years.[16] A fascinating flanking stone displays two suns. Above them is what is possibly the outline of a figure with a head and an uplifted arm. This figure is at the point of high summer (Figure 32).

At the top of the left of the border is the threefold sun circle (21 December, equinox, 21 June). Underneath the captive winter sun can be seen as a rhomboid drawn with double lines.

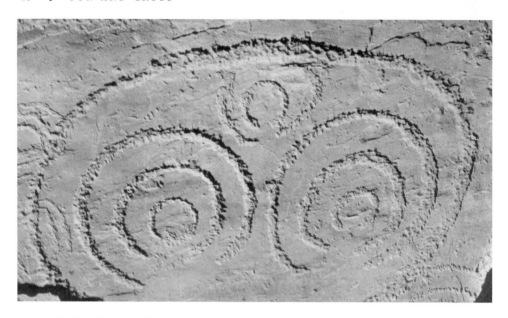

Figure 32. Detail from a stone in the circle around Knowth.

Figure 33. The tumulus of Knowth with the ring of stones.

Figure 34. Stone from the ring around Knowth.

Another flanking stone throws light on the phenomenon of perforated stones and menhirs. Before analysing it, certain ideas should be examined. Sacrifice to the sun was for the most part connected with a fire cult, since in both myth and cult, fire microcosmically symbolized the sun. This symbolic identification was world-wide and found clear, distinct forms in ancient Persia which influenced the Parsees of India. For the Greeks it was Prometheus who gave the fire of the sun to men. Solstice fires have been widespread at the summer and winter solstices throughout Northern Europe. Today primitive peoples still light fires by twisting a wooden stick on to a plank or a piece of wood.

Where would the fire of the sun be lit more in accord with the cult than on the sacred stone? Using a wooden pole the fire was drilled out of the ritual stone itself. In the course of time and after constant repetition the twisting pole deepened the pivot hole and a new position was chosen. In this way stones acquired a multitude of drill holes. Significantly these drill holes are very often found in the centre of a chiselled sun image. Thus the fire was drilled out of the sun symbol itself.

A stone on which the sun signs with drill holes can be clearly seen is the stone at Coolnaharragill, County Kerry (Figure 35).[17] But a flanking stone at Knowth with

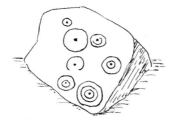

Figure 35. Stone at Coolnaharragill, County Kerry.

particularly beautiful finish and symbols displays the drill hole in the middle of radiating sun rays, and above is a second drill hole (Figure 34). Both have been placed on the vertical face of the stone and are therefore not bowls.

The fire drill was known in the distant past to the people of different continents. It was worked by hand with a bow or a cord. In the mountain districts of Switzerland what was presumably an old Celtic sun-custom was observed into the nineteenth century. 'In Appenzell and Luzern the spring fire was lit with a fire drill.'[18] A. Bertrand reports similar customs in Scotland and Sweden, in which inflammable resin was often used in addition.

An interesting opinion supports the existence of this custom. At the Council of Toulouse in AD 681 the Fathers of the Church criticized the heathen custom of lighting stone fires.

Drill holes and cup stones

An unusual, upright stone with drill holes is illustrated by J.C. Spahni.[19] It is La Pierre Schacran (Figure 36) at Gimel (Canton Vaud, Switzerland). It is suggested that the twelve months of the year's course are portrayed by the rising and falling curve formed by the twelve principal holes. Now this stone has two additional small holes directly above the fifth (May?) and between the sixth and seventh (June, July?). They may correspond to the Celtic festival of the first of May, Beltane, on which the spring

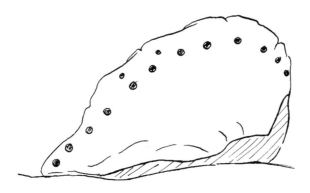

Figure 36. La Pierre Schacran at Gimel (Canton Vaud, Switzerland).

Figure 37a.

Figure 37b.

fire of purification was lit, and to the solstice on June 21. As the sun's power to affect nature continues to be experienced until the season when the fruit ripens at the end of September, these drill holes may then express the steep descent of October, November and December into winter cold. This, though, is only suggested as a possible hypothesis.

As well as the fire drill holes in the ritual stones, which for the most part have been made on vertical or slanting stone surfaces and which are erroneously termed cup or shell stones, there are also genuine flat, horizontal cup-marked stones (*bullauns*). They resemble basins (Figure 37a); food or a liquid can be placed in them. In the drill holes (*bolders*, Figure 37b) this cannot be done, since the stone is vertical. It can only be a drill hole with or without a sun ring.

In Ireland there are numerous genuine cup-marked stones. Particularly impressive is the tortoise-shaped Clonfinlough Stone, County Offaly.[20]

L. Rütimeyer reports that at Niederbronn (Vosges, France) women who wish to be mothers carry water at night to the cup-marked stones in the mountains.[21] They sprinkle the stones with the water and place gifts (sacrifices) in the cups.

In Switzerland, especially in the mountains where Celtic customs and traditions have survived for a long time, there is evidence that cup stones were used in performing sacrifices. E. Frick[22] reports that in Lötschental (Canton Valais) the stone cups are called *Papatollen*. In the local dialect *papp* means meal-pap, and 'tollen'

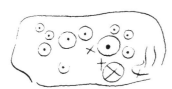

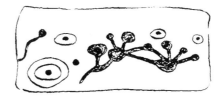

Figure 38. Alp Cotter, (Valais, Switzerland).

Figure 39. Gortboy, (County Kerry).

Figure 40. Clonfinlough Stone, County Offaly.

means hollow. Until the twentieth century it was the custom there to mix flour with water and to place it in such stone cups as a sacrifice of food for the spirits of nature and for the dead.

Jacot reports from the mountain hut of Basodino (Canton Ticino) that Alpine people used secretly to place sacrificial gifts in cup-marked stones to put the spirit of the mountain in a benevolent mood.[23] The stone at Alp Cotter (Evolène, Canton Valais) (Figure 38) is not unlike the Irish stone at Coolnaharragill. Here too the cups are surrounded by sun circles. The cup-marked stone at Gortboy (County Kerry) has cups joined by grooves (Figure 39).[24]

Summing up, it can be stated that in the drill holes and in the genuine cup-marked stones there are additional items of Stone Age ritual which indicate that communication with the world of the spirits and with nature was sought by means of fire and offerings of food. As fire won from the drill holes of the sacred stones served the union with the powers of light in the sun, in the cosmos and in the world of the divine, so did the offering of food serve the neighbourhood spirits of nature and the souls of the dead.

3. The Secret of the Spirals

Spirals are found as a prominent symbol in the tumuli of Newgrange and Knowth. They appear in other places too. Their dynamic can be better understood if ritual pacing and dancing are seen as the model for these symbols. A movement figure implies experience of the form. Compared with the spiral the circle at first seems a static, geometric shape. In the ritual dance the circle can move clockwise and anti-clockwise, can contract and expand. The spiral on the other hand is a shape that is already in uninterrupted movement. It links a peripheral outside with the centre and it links a centre with an unbounded surround, with universal space.

The mythical Greek Daedalus carved the Cretan labyrinth as a spiral on the gate of the temple in Cumae. Aeneas saw this when he set out on the journey to the underworld.[1] Daedalus was considered the founder of the spiral dance.[2]

It is known that in the Delian dance the leftward direction of the spiral was the path of death, while the direction to the right was thought of as the path of birth. The direction of movement was vitally important, not just the shape.

John Layard reports spiral dances connected with cults of the dead.[3] He describes how the cult of the dead is carried out on the island of Malekula in the New Hebrides in a district which has many dolmens and menhirs similar to those found in Ireland. On their deathward journey the dead travel along the spiral path. The living can achieve contact with them through the spiral dance. Today the people of Malekula still dance the Stone Age spiral dance.

In widely differing epochs the spiral was an important symbol, and it made its way into sacred architecture. Consequently the graves of Etruscan kings frequently have the shape of a spiral or coiled mound. Dante's purgatory, the path of purification in the realm of the dead, is a spiral hill. The steps leading up to the Babylonian ziggurat, the temple sanctuary, were spiral in shape. All these ritual spiral buildings and paths indicate the way of contemplation, of spirtualization as well as the path into the life after death and the macrocosm.

Here an observation made by the brilliant mathematician Jakob Bernoulli can be mentioned. He thought a great deal about the meaning of the spiral, and asked for one to be placed on his own tombstone as a symbol. He observed that the infolding spiral sweeps into finite space from the infinite and eternal, while when it unfolds it returns from finite space to the infinite. It is a symbol of the threshold between space and spacelessness, time and eternity, materialization and spiritualization.

The basis for the totality of the spiral is the polarity of the inner and the outer, (sweeping out and sweeping in again). Spiral movement is the dynamic of polarity. It is therefore the image of life and death, the image of everything rhythmical, of becoming and passing away.

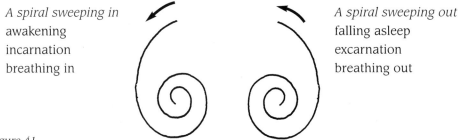

A spiral sweeping in
awakening
incarnation
breathing in

A spiral sweeping out
falling asleep
excarnation
breathing out

Figure 41.

Goethe discovered the spiral dance in the plant world as a rule for their growth into the light. We know the way beans climb up spirally, the spiral organization of the leaves of many plants as they climb on the stem, the spiral structure of many types of seed (fir-cones) and flowers.[4]

Mythic man moved and danced to these patterns in rotation as the path of life (moving to the right) and the path of death (moving to the left). The threshold stone before the entrance to the tumulus at Newgrange has an impressive display of these two directions as reversing spirals: the path of life joined to the path of death (Figure 20).

The upper half of the threshold stone is divided into two parts by a vertical bar. In the left half three path of life spirals can be seen which in reverse become paths of death. In the right half there are two paths of death spirals which in the centre change and resemble paths of life. The lively rhythm of the spirals is interspersed with rhomboid sun images. When such spiral patterns were danced or walked, it was the rhythm of becoming and passing away that was enacted. It is at the same time the dance of both incarnation and excarnation; or it is in turn the evolutionary chain of earthly lives or the succession of the circles of the year. The spiral dance later found an ornamental form in the Greek meander pattern.

Figure 42.

Chain spiral dances of this kind stubbornly lived on in Europe into the nineteenth century. Ludwig Uhland[5] makes this report from the small town of Gruyères (Switzerland): 'One Sunday evening seven persons began a small ring dance on the Castle lawn at Gruyères which only stopped on Tuesday morning at Saanen; when seven hundred youths and girls had joined the line the total impression was of a spiral ring.'

What happened was that as more hands were linked and the line of people grew longer and longer a leader guided them into a centre and then out again. As a result an unending meander pattern came into existence. Relics of this spiral dance, originally a ritual dance, have survived in folk dances and children's games.

Not only in Scandinavia but also in England and Germany primitive rites are found with stones placed on the ground. On Åland (Ahvenanmaa, Finland) at certain times the *Jungfrudans* (virgins' dance) was danced on spiral stones in the twentieth century.[6]

The spiral is therefore a very instructive symbol because on the one hand its derivation from the ritual dance is proved again and again, while on the other hand we can still today experience in its movement something of its characteristic polarity.

Pre-Christian sun spirals

In Ireland megalithic engravings frequently display the three part sun ring *(a)*. This sun ring figure is identical with the three part sun arch *(b)*. The winter sun arch (December 21) is the lowest, the next arch above is for the equinoxes (March 21, September 23) and the highest above that is the summer arch (June 21). In *c* only the two main sun arches of the year are shown, the longest and the shortest day. To the right and left are the rising and the setting sun on the horizon.

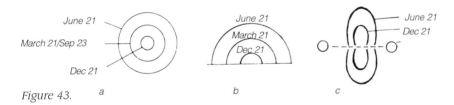

Figure 43.　　*a*　　　　　　　　　　*b*　　　　　　　　*c*

In the three circles of the static, threefold sun symbol the dynamic spiral form can be drawn from the centre to the circumference and with this the path of the sun from the winter point to the high summer position can be illustrated *(d)*. In *e* the entire course of the year is shown as a double spiral. On the left within the winter position it swings out over the summer arch to the next winter position. Then *f* shows *e* as a reversing spiral: circumference to centre (June 21 to December 21) and again from centre back to the circumference (December 21 to June 21).

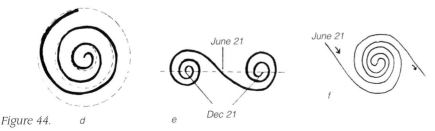

Figure 44.　　*d*　　　　　　　*e*　　　　　　*f*

A special document which in its style is unlike any other is the spiral stone at Turoe (County Galway, Figure 45). In character it resembles a central ritual stone reminiscent of the Omphalos at Delphi, the 'navel of the world' (Figure 46). It is a tall, dome-shaped granite stone about 1.5 metres (5 feet) in height, whose upper surface is covered with free spiral shapes. These are ornamental in style, but are scattered indiscriminately, so that the whole stone seems to be a mass of spirals.

The lower margin at the base is decorated with rectangular shapes, stiff, lifeless geometrical shapes in contrast to the animated dome. Which cult this stone once served remains a mystery. It guarded the secret of life and death. As it is dated in the third century BC it is of Celtic origin.[7] How extinguishably sun symbol and spiral, rhomboid and other things survived the march of time is a phenomenon we shall have to consider again in the case of early Christian Irish stone crosses in a later chapter. Here in Ireland it seems as though the megalithic and Celtic past tried to complete its metamorphosis into the Christian era intact.

Figure 45. Spiral stone of Turoe (County Galway).   *Figure 46. The Omphalos, 'navel of the world,' at Delphi.*

II

From Celtic to Early Christian Culture

4. The Original Population of Ireland

In the course of history Ireland's population has been affected by many invasions, in the same way as the population of the Continent has been affected by the movement of nations. A homogeneous nation cannot be said to have existed in pre-Christian times. On the contrary, according to C.S. Coon four layers of pre-Celtic inhabitants can be distinguished.

In the later Stone Age and probably in the Bronze Age also, Iberians pressed in from Spain and Western France. In the Bronze Age there was trade with Spain, France and Scandinavia. In the Wicklow Mountains Irish gold was mined and traded overseas. Archaeological discoveries record oil pitchers and lamps from Greece and pearl jewellery from Egypt. As early as before the sixth century BC seafaring Phoenicians travelled from the west of Asia through the Pillars of Hercules (Straits of Gibraltar) and reached Ireland. There is a reference to this in the legendary account, the Book of Invasions (*Cin of Drom-Snechte*) that in very ancient times the Milesians (inhabitants of Miletus on the coast of Asia Minor) had come over the sea to Ireland, where they were called the 'Sons of Milidh.' Ella Young quotes the legendary tradition of the journey of the Milesians:

> 'How got you knowledge of Ireland?' asked Ogma [the Irishman].
> 'O Champion,' answered Amergin [the Milesian], 'from the centre of the Great Plain there rises a tower of crystal. Its top pierces the heavens, and from the ramparts of it the wisest one among us got sight of this land. When he saw it his heart was filled with longing ... Therefore we set out to seek that land, and behold, we have come to it.'[1]

In a mythic image Ireland is here pictured as the island of desire.

The Celtic invasion

Between the third and fifth centuries BC the Celts settled in Ireland. The number and dates of their invasions are not known. The original home of the Celts is thought to have been the Upper Rhine (South-Western Germany, Northern Switzerland, Eastern France). At the beginning of the fifth century there was something like a Celtic belt which stretched from the Danube in Austria north of the Alps as far as Northern Spain. In the period following, a number of invasions were carried out from this belt into a number of countries (see the map overleaf).

In race and speech the Celts form a branch of the western Indo-Germanic

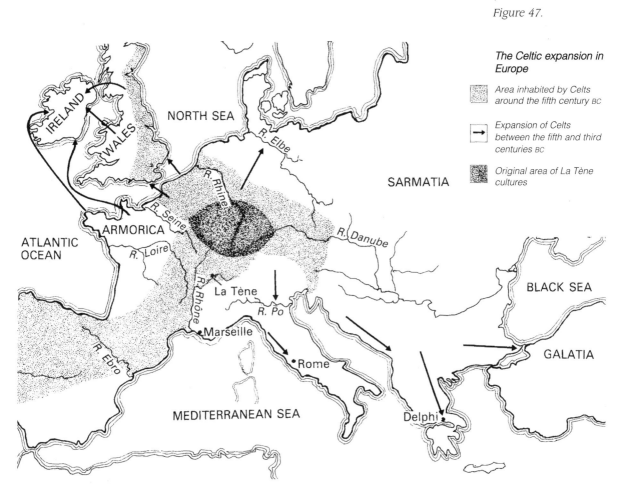

Figure 47.

The Celtic expansion in Europe

Area inhabited by Celts around the fifth century BC

Expansion of Celts between the fifth and third centuries BC

Original area of La Tène cultures

people, close to the Germanic people. Tall, blond or red-haired, blue-eyed, long headed — this is how they are described. Their name, *Keltoi*, those wearing clothes (old Irish Celtic for coat) points to a contrast with the half-naked original inhabitants of Central and Western Europe, who were not Indo-European. The routes of their eastward migration (to the Danube and down as far as the Black Sea, to Greece, to the Balkans, to Italy and eventually to Spain and Portugal) brought a disturbing, unsettling element into the peoples they overran in pre-Christian times. After the Celts had penetrated all France and the great part of the northern Iberian peninsula their invasions branched off to cross the sea to Britain and Ireland. Although their numbers were small in Ireland their active national temperament led to a Celtic character being imposed on the island, despite the old established tribes there. These latter were retarded by a megalithic culture.

It should be mentioned that the Celts always showed great consideration for existing religions and cult centres. They honoured existing religious traditions and gradually absorbed them into their own culture. In Ireland they called themselves 'Goidil,' from which comes the later Irish name 'Gael.' Old megalithic sacred places in Ireland experienced a revival under the Celts. It is not known when prehistoric structures were incorporated in Celtic mythology.'

Symbiosis of this sort could occur in the religious sphere in those times because no intellectually restrictive creed or philosophy served as a divisive factor. On the contrary, varied forms of ritual and religious practice pointed to the same experience of the ever-present and active gods. Accordingly Rolleston states quite correctly:

> What is quite clear is that when the Celts got to Western Europe they found there a people with a powerful priesthood, a ritual, and imposing religious monuments ... The inferences, as I read the facts, seem to be that Druidism in its essential features was imposed upon the imaginative and sensitive nature of the Celt ... by the earlier population of Western Europe, among the Megalithic People ...[2]

It is therefore possible to speak of a pre-Celtic and a Celtic culture coexisting in Ireland. In order to understand the three or four centuries BC in Ireland after the Celtic invasions it is necessary to realize some other essential elements of Celtic culture. Above all there is the question of the spiritual leadership of the people carried out by the druids, to whom the supreme authority was entrusted.

The Celtic scholar Jan de Vries[3] decisively rejects the reduction of the Celtic Druids to mere soothsayers: '... this is characteristic of a tendency in theology that appears to be always ready to recognize the primitive only, and to reinterpret late and degenerate phenomena as original conceptions.'

The Druid as a trained initiate is also called *cerunnes* (stag) in Celtic Northern Europe. R. Grosse gives an explanation of the meaning of the pictures on the cauldron at Gundestrop.[4] Convincingly he points out that the stages of the initiation rites of Celtic Druids are here symbolized. For instance, the antlers sprouting from the Druid's head as he meditates are an image of spiritual connection with the cosmos. The important link between sun and moon motifs is also here. On the head of the ritual stag there is the open, cosmic triangle at the top, and under it the sun swastika, whose ray plunges down into the moon's sickle-shaped basin. This reveals a relationship between Celtic and Stone Age cult symbolism in Ireland (central stone at Slieve na Caillighe). This juxtaposition possibly indicates that in Ireland the Celts felt that they were connected with the age-old cult of the sun and its symbolism.

Julius Caesar shows great respect for the knowledge and training of the Celtic

Druids: 'Report says that in the schools of the Druids they learn by heart a great number of verses, and therefore some persons remain twenty years under training.'[5] Another Roman, Pomponius Mela reports: 'The training is long and secret. It is carried out in caves and forests.'[6]

Tradition attributes scholarly and superior abilities to the Druids, including an intermittent atavistic power of supersensory perception, linked with a gift for prophecy. 'Clairvoyance is widely recognized and its incidence is usually preceded by the verb *adciu*, "see" — i.e. with my eye of inner vision: "I see red, I see very red".'[7]

They also practised the art of healing, which was connected with knowledge of nature cure and suggestive magic. The Druids kept their knowledge of people, earth and cosmos secret, as was usual in all the ancient mysteries. In the time of Vespasian, Dio Chrysostom remarked that their leadership was also decisive in earthly matters: 'The king could not take decisions without them, ... the kings are servants of their ideas.' Accordingly the first to speak in assemblies was the Druid, then the king, and only after them the people.[8]

The Greek historian Diodorus Siculus (in Julius Caesar's time) says of the Celts: 'The Celts hold the doctrine of Pythagoras that the souls of men are immortal and that after a predetermined number of years the soul returns again to life, and enters another body.'[9]

Three grades of priestly training were distinguished. Firstly the leading Druids had the power of participating in government decisions which has been mentioned. Secondly the *filid*, to whom prophetic powers were attributed, were active as judges in Ireland. (The oldest fragments of ancient Irish laws are written in verse form, and date from the sixth and seventh centuries.)[10] Thirdly, as wandering singers and story-tellers the bards had the task of sustaining the vitality of the myth among the people.

The best of them enjoyed rights of hospitality at the king's court. An old saying states 'the king should go with the singer,' which was a way of saying that what the bard sang about him was important for the reputation of the king. The king had to stay in harmony with the bard. It was reported in an old Irish chronicle (Senchus Môr) that the senior bard, called *ollam*, could recite 350 stories, the junior bard only seven. There was an *ollam* still in the sixth Christian century. He was accompanied by about thirty pupils and in this fashion conducted a wandering bardic school.[11]

This phenomenon clearly shows that the pre-Christian bardic organization was projected undiminished into the Christian era and continued to function as we have already seen was the case with symbols and folk custom. 'This is the ancient native civilization of Ireland with her traditions intact from the Iron Age, like an unwritten manuscript of the ancient Celtic world.'[12]

There were already in the sixth century a significant number of Christian monasteries who to some extent had entered into relationships with bardic schools. We learn from Columban that he too had passed through a bardic schooling before he submitted to monastic education. Old, pre-Christian myths about gods and heroes existed harmoniously side by side with the new, Christian teaching of the post-Christian bards. This is another indication of how completely old Irish Christianity was absorbed into Celtic Druidism and the bardic system. In this the almost incredibly tolerant attitude of Celtic culture is revealed, and its willingness to accept, integrate and cultivate other spiritual traditions. Accordingly in the tenth century the bard Forgell is said to have recited a saga at the court of the Ulster Chief Mongam every evening from the beginning of November until May 1. In the surviving catalogue classical material is also entered — the *Iliad*, the *Odyssey*, epics about Alexander — although the catalogue consists mainly of Celtic sagas from the pre-Christian era.[13]

The bards were givers of both advice and warnings to the tribal chiefs and to the people. They kindled courage and enthusiasm, praised and eulogized, soothed passions and mocked weaknesses. In this way they stimulated a human conscience. In the same way as the Druid priest gave a positive content to the religious feasts, the bard gave content to the worldly feasts and banquets. He was able to clothe the mythic content in a brightly coloured robe. He built bridges from the past into the present, from the supersensory to the sensory, and in this way approached his most important task: to prepare men for the spiritual in their thoughts and dreams.

Gonzague de Reynold, an enthusiastic authority on Celtic customs, describes the Celts as poets, priests and warriors rather than visual artists. Their world remains spiritual and rarely takes a material form. They have gods who have no need of visual arts. They live in nature, in the soul, in breath, in word and song. The spiritual nature of Celtic religion gave the Celts greater readiness to accept Christianity than the Teutons.

Obviously this fact in large measure accounts for the Old Irish and Celtic situation and its metamorphosis into Christianity. In contrast to Ireland Celtic culture in France and Britain was overcome by the Romans, and the centres of its mysteries systematically destroyed. Ireland remained the only Celtic country which the Romans did not penetrate. As a result only here was a genuine meeting of Christianity with an intact Celtic and Druid culture possible.

Ireland at the time of the birth of Christ

It was a stroke of luck for the history of the world that the Romans did not annex Ireland. Tacitus reports an invasion that was considered but not carried out: 'I have often heard Agricola say ... that Ireland could be invaded and conquered with one legion and a moderate number of auxiliaries.'[15]

Agricola, who was Roman Governor and Commander in Britain from about AD 59 to 84, believed reports about the bad reputation of the seas around Ireland and statements that they were only navigable for a few days in the year. The Romanization of the island was therefore abandoned as a result of these rumours which were perhaps deliberately spread from Ireland. A considerable number of coastal fortification are known, which form a hedgehog defence round the island. So Ireland, which was also protected in those days by the strength of the spirit of the Druids, was able to make the Romans fear an uncertain adventure across the sea, the risks of which they were unwilling to face.

On the surface Ireland at this time was divided into a motley throng of tribal regions, each with its tribal king, who in turn was a vassal of the king of the province. There were four ancient provinces: Ulaid (Ulster), Connachta (Connaught), Laigin (Leinster) and Mumu (Munster). High kingship came into existence later (c. AD 279–405). Land was originally communal property, and the king only had the usufruct of certain estates for the period of their office. The earth and the herds were abundant and hunger was unknown.

Certain families received parts of the common arable land in exchange for an undertaking to have the most suitable of their offspring in each generation trained as a 'scholar' (Druid, later priest). There are many witnesses to the primacy enjoyed by the spiritual life in Old Ireland. 'The countless honours and privileges enjoyed from the earliest times by men of art and science show clearly that the Gaels were a high-minded race, with an appreciation of mental culture rare indeed among people on a similar, comparatively primitive level of material civilization.'[15]

On the Emerald Isle, where conflict with the world outside ceased at the time of the birth of Christ, a peace that lasted for centuries, the creative capacity of Celtic culture was able to develop its activity and its spiritual influence in an epoch of peace. In a further development it was to experience in a surprisingly short time the penetration of Christianity.

Some motifs from Celtic mythology

In his fundamental study of Celtic religion Jan de Vries attempted to bring some clarity into the wealth, or indeed confusion, of Celtic divinities. In doing so he relied a great deal on Roman sources. The Romans, however, interpreted these strange gods all too quickly as equivalents of their Roman and Greek Olympic Pantheon. If a god were associated with lightning, he was immediately termed a 'Celtic Jupiter.' If light was worshipped, this indicated a cult of Apollo. It is certainly possible to perceive an affinity between Apollo and the Celtic Belenos, between Jupiter and Dagda, between Lugh and Odin. Observation of resemblances of this kind, however, rather blurs the outline and character of the Celtic gods. The Celt in worshipping them gazed through them on the creative forces in nature, universe and man. Ella Young, Irish by birth, who had still heard the Gaelic story tellers, the Shanachie, in the last century, gives a vivid poetic description of some Celtic deities. A great deal of the spirit and imaginative strength of the Celtic imagination can be experienced in her writing. She tells of the sun warrior, Lugh, who was to help in Ireland to overcome the dark Fomors, who darken the earth with their shadows.

> [Mananaun, the sea god, said] 'I will set you on my own white horse and give you companions who are as high-hearted as yourself. I will put my helmet on your head and my breastplate over your heart: you shall drive the Fomorians out of Ireland as chaff is driven by the wind.'
>
> When Lugh put on the helmet of Mananaun, brightness shot into the sky as if a new sun had risen; when he put on the breast-plate, a great wave of music swelled and sounded through Tir-nan-Oge; when he mounted the white horse, a mighty wind swept past him, and lo! the companions Mananaun had promised [the De Danaans] rode beside him.
>
> They took their weapons and went to the Hill of Usna, and they were not long on it when a band of Fomorian devastators came upon them.
>
> ... Scarcely had the weapons clashed when a light appeared in the horizon and a sound of mighty battle trumpets shook the air. The light was so white that no one could look at it, and great rose-red streamers shot from it into the sky ....
>
> Out of the light came the glorious company of warriors from Tir-nan-Oge. Lugh was leading them.[16]

When centuries later the Christian figure of the Archangel Michael was portrayed in battle against the world of fallen demons, it was possible for Lugh's battle to be resurrected in Christian dress. Significantly, Michael was highly honoured in Celtic Christianity.

Another aspect of the Irish Celtic sun god was shown by Ogma whose full name Grian-Aiench means 'with a face of the sun.' He is the word of God, the Logos, the inspirer of poetry and speech. Later he is also the creator of writing (Ogham script), honoured for recording words. This joining together of the words Logos and sun will be encountered again in the early period of Irish Christianity.

Celtic annual festivals

It is understandable that a people like the Celts, for whom the sun was the embodiment of the highest divinity, was able without conflict to enter and share in a common culture with the original population of Ireland, who practised the megalithic cult of the sun. It is astonishing that the megalithic festivals of the sun, which we know from the layout of the 'alignments' of Brittany, meet us again in complete similarity in the Celtic annual festival.

After the darkness of winter the festival of purification, Imbolc, was held. The sun grew in strength again, the corn sown in winter began to sprout. Ritual washing was carried out in connection with certain customs when eating.[17]

Ploughs and tools were blessed. Dancing by the women aimed to accelerate the growth of the flax, a fertility round dance in honour of the increasing power of the sun. In the period of conversion to Christianity Imbolc was replaced by Candlemas when candlelight processions took place. In Ireland in particular Imbolc developed into the Feast of St Bride.

The fertility of the sun revealed itself in the abundant variety of spring. In its honour the festival of Beltane was celebrated. May trees, May sun wheels and processions around the fields have survived in folk custom. The word is made up from two elements: *Bel* is the sun god Belenos, *tane* means fire. At Beltane the fires of the sun god blazed. People leapt over them, singly or in pairs, and drove the cattle between two fires to purify them.

Lugnasad (Lammas in England), the main festival of the year, was celebrated in the middle of August, that is at the beginning of the harvest. The sun god had poured abundance of light on the fields and had ripened the corn. Heaven and earth had mated to bring this about. Lugnasad is a compound word meaning 'wedding feast of the sun god Lugh'. The Earth Mother gave birth to the divine fruit, the corn. There are references to rituals at Lugnasad in which there was a burial mound (tumulus) of the Earth Mother in the centre of the festival site.[18]

On this day marriages were concluded. There were great feasts accompanied by horse and chariot races. There is evidence of the festival still being held at Tara in AD 560 which indicates the coexistence and mutual toleration of the Celtic and the Christian.[19]

Samhain was a festival connected with darkness and the night. The light in the night from November 1 onwards, was Sirius, the 'dancing star decked with plumes' of Irish sagas.[20] He led the round dance of the stars, the powers of the gloomy underworld rose up and moved over the frosty, bare, dark earth. Samhain means union. Even the upper gods were in the air on their way to meet with the lower gods and the gloomy powers of the deep. There they forged the seeds of sparks for new light which could not be banished by the gloom of winter. In Ireland all fires on hearths throughout the island were extinguished and rekindled by a fire ritually lit at Tlachtga so that warmth and light should not vanish when cold and darkness attacked.[21] Samhain was also associated with sacrifice to acquire a new control of the good gods that was the essential, basic idea of all these festivals, the idea of continually renewing the bond between man and god.

5. The Beginnings of Old Irish Christianity

The beginning of Christianity is one of the major problems of Irish history, as original documents of the early Christian period no longer exist. Ludwig Bieler[1] accordingly says bluntly: 'We do not know when or in what way the Irish first came into contact with Christianity.'

This assertion is positive in its rejection of the fiction that St Patrick was the first person to introduce Christianity into Ireland and who made it flourish there, and that this was Roman Christianity. This fiction has been obstinately maintained for too long for purposes of ecclesiastical politics. This is given as the origin of old Irish Christianity in many historical works and encyclopedias. It is untrue. Irish Christianity existed before Patrick. Later we shall examine his influence. It is proposed to summarize some references now.

Precedents in Celtic mythology

There was among the Celts a cult of worship of a triune god. There are repeated references to three-headed gods. J. Moreau mentions thirty of them.[2] The triple-head in the Irish National Museum in Dublin has the rough finish which was a Celtic characteristic and it is not easy to interpret. Rather more is expressed by the statue of a triune god on the Magdalenenberg at Klagenfurt (Austria) where there was a big Celtic town. One of its components can be recognized as feminine, and has breasts. This stone image was taken into the hillside chapel in Christian times, possibly under the influence of Irish missionaries. In the centre of the three heads a bowl had been hollowed out which was used to hold holy water. The statue is an expressive symbol for the self-sacrifice of Celtic culture and the transition to Christianity.

In Ireland Tanaros worshipped as God the Father. God the Son, Lugh (god of light, also called Beli) was at the same time god of fire because fire to the Irish is the earthly likeness of the sun. The third god was the divine virgin Brigantia (Brigit). This triple form indicates an affinity with the Christian Trinity. Celtic culture in its highest religious expression approached close to Christianity.

Immediately before the appearance of Christianity Druidism was at the height of its power and development. It is a phenomenon of the greatest importance that in the first Christian centuries assimilation into the earliest form of Christianity was carried out in Ireland not only without struggle and antagonism, but with peaceful coexistence. J. Pokorny remarks in this connection:

> In the whole word there is scarcely another example of heathen epics
> being written down in the monasteries several hundred years after the

introduction of Christianity; yet this was the case in Ireland; the loving labour of the monks handed down in countless manuscripts, stories such as, for example, 'The Cattle Raid of Cooley', (*Táin Bó Cuailnge*) which tells of the deeds of Cú Chulainn, the legendary hero of Ulster, in a battle against the whole of the rest of Ireland. These stories give us a very accurate picture of the civilization of pre-Christian, and indeed to some extent, of pre-Aryan, times.[3]

Françoise Henry comes to a similar conclusion concerning the artistic remains of the period: 'In Ireland where Christianity entered without conflict, the conversion was carried out very gently ... the result of this fusion is unique. Up to a certain point in its early stages Irish art is paradoxical, a heathen art which slipped into an ecclesiastical art.'[4]

But since the art is an expression of spirituality we have here a clear demonstration of how heathen spirituality 'slipped into' Christian spirituality and vice versa. This singular symbiosis is produced which distinguishes early Christian Irish art and which we shall observe in fragments of the liturgy.

Had the Eastern Church any part?

Todd produces numerous examples of monks in early Christian Ireland living in groups of seven.[5] This does not necessarily imply an imitation of the Eastern Church as communities of seven of this sort were common in Irish and Celtic Druidism. On the other hand there is direct evidence of connection with Christian Egypt. In *Félire Óenguso* seven Egyptian monks are mentioned who lived in Ireland at Disert Vlidh (also Figure 48).

Figure 48. Seven Egyptian Monks. Detail of the northern cross at Ahenny (County Tipperary).

The old Irish custom of storing water for Epiphany (January 6, Baptism of Christ) and of lighting Easter fires and letting them burn all through the year (the fire ritual of Kildare) was also a custom of the Eastern Church. Then it must be made clear that early on the Old Irish calculation of the date of Easter agreed with the Eastern Church. This later developed into a significant contrast with the Church of Rome.

Delius points out further areas of agreement:

> The practice of Egyptian monks of separating into groups of several brothers when singing psalms is also found in the Irish Church. Variant readings in the Gospel which were used in the Irish Church can also be traced back to the Eastern Church. In the book known as the Book Dimma, an Irish manuscript of the Gospel of the seventh or eighth century, Coptic variant readings are found ... the rejection of all human systems which is constantly found with the Irish saints, is found also with the Eastern monks.[6]

Whatever traces of Christian contact across the trade routes of the sea may occasionally come to light, such contacts would never have been strong enough to convert an old established, spiritually active order of Druids (which the Celtic Druids were) to Christianity, and in a relatively short time to cause them to found such a number of Christian centres and monasteries, as are already found in the first Christian centuries.

The appearance of Pelagius in Southern Europe

Towards the end of the fourth century the Irish scholar and itinerant preacher Pelagius enters history in Rome as the philosophical expounder of an independent Christianity. He spoke Latin and Greek fluently, was a brilliant orator and is a powerful witness of the high level of spiritual education in Ireland and in its monastic culture before the advent of Patrick. Chapter 11 deals with his great importance as an early missionary in the Mediterranean region.

The fact that in Rome before Patrick's time Pope Celestine I was aware of Irish Christianity is shown by his sending Palladius in AD 431 to Ireland as bishop, with the object (according to Prosper of Aquitaine) of administering the sacraments to 'the Irish who professed Christ.' There were therefore at this time (before Patrick) a sufficient number of Christians in Ireland to make this attempt to win over the independent mood for the Church of Rome. This attempt was a failure and had no after-effects. Palladius died on the homeward journey.

Ludwig Bieler comments on this undertaking:

> It is tempting to connect this step with another, taken by the same Pope on the suggestion of Palladius — namely the mission to Britain in 429 of the Bishops Germanus and Lupus. This mission also was recorded in

Prosper's chronicle. Palladius ... at that time was a deacon of the Church of Rome ...[7]

Plans for the systematic Christianization [Romanization!] of Ireland might very well have been made about that time. A possible reference to such plans is a satirical poem ....

> Adze-head will come,
> Across the bold-headed sea,
> Hollow-head his mantle
> Bent-head his staff,
> His table facing east,
> His people, chanting, answer:
> Amen, amen.

This was perhaps sung by bards all over the country in the fifth century as a comment on the Roman enterprise.

Patrick's contribution

In a letter which has been preserved, and which is acknowledged to be genuine, Patrick writes to a certain Coroticus (fifth century): 'In the days of old the law of God was well planted and propagated in Ireland; I do not wish to take credit for the work of my predecessors; I share the task with all those whom God has called and fore-ordained to preach the Gospel.'[8] Walter Delius takes this point and declares, 'From his letter to Coroticus the conclusion can be drawn that Patrick supposed that the Christians he found already there in Ireland had come to Christianity of *their own accord* (author's italics).[9]

This can hardly be understood in any other way than as evidence of inspired or visionary experiences, and this would also correspond with legendary reports. In the *Vita* by Tírechán the statement is made that Patrick found that there were already churches and monasteries in Ireland.

The evidence of myths and sagas

There are some accounts which say that Irish Druids possessed second sight and learned details of Christ's mission and passion through spiritual vision. Accordingly J. Keating refers to the legend of King Conchobar, to whom a Druid in a trance is said to have spoken about the sun's darkening on Good Friday and the death of Christ.

A story is told about the Chief Druid of Iona that when dying he had a vision of Brigit with the child Jesus, rocking him on her knees as he slept. A very old legend says about Brigit that a Christian seer on first meeting her cried out: 'This is Mary, whom I see; because I recognize in exact detail her figure and appearance.' So Brigit came to be worshipped as Maria Hibernorum.[10]

Occult research

In his reports on the Akashic Record Rudolf Steiner made some comments on ancient Irish cult centres and their relationship to Christianity:

> Strictly guarded were these Mysteries of Hibernia, hidden in an atmosphere of intense earnestness. There they stood in the centuries before the Mystery of Golgotha, and there they remained at the time of the Mystery of Golgotha. Over in Asia the Mystery of Golgotha took place; in Jerusalem the events came to pass that were later made known to men in the Gospels by the way of tradition. But in the moment when the tragedy of the Mystery of Golgotha was being enacted in Palestine, in that very moment it was known and beheld clairvoyantly in the Mysteries of Hibernia. No report was brought by word of mouth, no communication whatever was possible; but in the Mysteries of Hibernia the event was fulfilled in a symbol, in a picture, at the same time that it was fulfilled in actual fact in Jerusalem. Men came to know of it, not through tradition but by a spiritual path. Whilst in Palestine that most majestic and sublime event was being enacted in concrete physical reality, — over in Hibernia, in the Mysteries, the way had been so prepared through the performance of certain rites that at the very time when the Mystery of Golgotha was fulfilled, a living picture of it was present in the astral light.[11]

By a different approach the French historian Alexandre Bertrand came to a similar opinion concerning the part played by the Druids in the introduction of Christianity into Ireland. At any rate Bertrand assumed that Christian missionaries from the Eastern Church had come to Ireland and convinced the leading Druids, and that thereupon these had gone over to Christianity and the people had followed them. There is no historical tradition concerning these missionaries but Bertrand is only able to explain the rapid and unopposed spread of Christianity by assuming the co-operation of the Druids. Steiner considers that this co-operation was based on the inspired clairvoyant experiences of leading Druids.

Christianity before Patrick

The historical and mythological references which have been summarized in the preceding sections show that Christianity was certainly established in Ireland before Patrick, and that the Druids and the bards had a part in a Christianity characterized by Celtic emblems. The pre-Christian Celtic bards gradually developed a Christian content. Probably there were contacts with the Eastern Church and with Coptic Christianity (Egypt). For centuries these two movements were linked with each other. The Druid order bit by bit developed into an order of monks and priests of a Christian character. In both creed and ritual this old Irish Christianity came into existence completely independent of Rome. It gradually developed its own independent Christian ritual and liturgy. It entered into the life of the people of Ireland without fixed dogmas or any striving for ecclesiastical power. This is the reason why in this early period there were no martyrs and no religious feuds. It could be said that until the fifth and sixth centuries there was a period of gradual consolidation and inner growth which culminated in the flourishing monastic culture of Columcille's time (sixth century). From now on Ireland was thought of on the Continent as 'the Island of Saints'. The wealth of Christian culture in the seventh and eighth centuries created that spiritual inclination towards the northern part of the Continent which inspired Ireland to Christianize it. There was no rigidly defined doctrine or any desire to organize in any ecclesiastical sense, but a movement borne along by enthusiasm and religious zeal which boldly spread news of the advent of the incarnate Logos as the 'new testament' and taught the forms of human relationship that accorded with this.

6. The Tradition of the Nordic Bards and its Transformation into Christian Forms

The most important and virtually the only medium for communication of mythic man was the word. Priest and bard communicated with the people with words; with words fashioned images, conjured up the past and deeds of the gods; with words sang of the heroic deeds of men. The ceremonial word in conjunction with signs permeated the ritual and made it possible to turn to the gods in prayer. In the form of a magic word (mantram) it was spoken into the ascending smoke of sacrifice, to carry requests and thanks alike. Again as a magic word it was used by the priestly healer as a blessing of the wound to promote healing. Apart from ritual the word was important in every sphere of life as 'rune language', of which folklore of later times has abundant evidence. There were blood runes, sleep runes, hunt and battle runes, love runes, and so on. The Nordic *Erik Saga* describes how a group of thirty people using runes sang a woman into a trance in order to obtain a message.[1] On the island of Iona the fishermen had a 'iorram', a song with which they lured seals.[2]

Certain gods were worshipped as creators of speech, the arts of language and music. For the Teutons Odin was father of the 'speaking tongue', the outward flowing of creative breath. Accordingly his head was still displayed in Norwegian stave churches and in Romanesque and Lombard churches.[3]

Among the Celts Ogma was worshipped as the word god. Lugh, the god of the sun, was at the same time creator of the word, of the arts and of music. Mythology

Figure 49. Odin with 'the outward flowing of creative breath'.

provides a testament to his influence. One evening Lugh played on Dagda's harp before King Nuda:

> Lugh played the music of joy, and outside the dun the birds began to sing as though it were morning and wonderful crimson flowers sprang through the grass ...
>
> Lugh played the music of sorrow. The wind moaned outside ... The De Danaans within the dun bowed their heads on their hands and wept ...
>
> Lugh played the music of peace, and outside there fell silently a strange snow ... Flake by flake the quiet of the Land of the Silver Fleece settled in the hearts and minds ... [4]

The Roman writer Lucan (AD 39–65) reported that he saw a picture of the Celtic god Ogma, and from his tongue came slender golden chains with amber pearls which hung on the ears of human forms. The head on one capital of the stave church at Hurum recalls this.

The most famous Irish bard is Ossian (Irish Oisín), son of Finn, (Finn MacCumhail) the hero of the southern Irish epic cycle. In the course of time there arose the mythical image of the aged blind singer Ossian, the herald of antiquity. The Ossianic Society in Dublin published Irish Ossianic texts (1854–61). Real interest in Ossian and the world of the northern bards was roused in the eighteenth century. James Macpherson in his *Fragments of Ancient Poetry Collected in the Highlands* and in his *Fingal,* published romanticized bardic poetry. He was inspired by versions which were ordinarily preserved in Scotland but which he expanded to such an extent that their genuineness was contested. These lyrics greatly influenced Herder, Goethe and the German romantic movement. Although Macpherson was accused of forgery, he had indeed unquestionably included some genuine bardic material in his work. Here is a sample passage from Ossian's Works by James Macpherson:

> Daughter of heaven, fair art thou! the silence of thy face is pleasant! Thou comest forth in loveliness. The stars attend thy blue course in the east. The clouds rejoice in thy presence, O moon! They brighten their dark-brown sides. Who is like thee in heaven, light of the silent night? The stars are ashamed in they presence. They turn away their sparkling eyes. Whither dost thou retire from they course, when the darkness of thy countenance grows? Hast thou thy hall, like Ossian? Dwellest thou in the shadow of grief? Have thy sisters fallen from heaven? Are they who rejoiced with thee, at night, no more? ....[5]

Figure 50. Odin, the father of the 'speaking tongue', the outward flowing of creative breath. Capital in the church at Hurum, Norway.

Druid elements

The Graeco-Roman historian and geographer Strabo (*c*. 63 BC – *c*. AD 24) who travelled a great deal in his life and was well-informed, reported that there were three classes of spiritual leaders among the Celts, among whom he included the bards. This was his classification of the three classes:

The *Druids* are occupied with the study of nature and with ethics. They are considered to be the most just. They are also active as judges and peacemakers between armies.

The *vates* organize the sacrifices and investigate nature.

The *bards* are poets and singers of hymns.

Strabo still knew that the bards were a priestly guild. As wandering teachers of the people they imbued their souls with songs, myths and legends in order to stimulate and cultivate a moral sensitivity and an inner life. They are mentioned as counsellors and people who utter warnings. In war they came forward to create courage and inspire warriors to fight bravely. They gave a mythic background, gay or thoughtful, to every worldly gathering. They were the real guides and creators of the people's sense of right and wrong, they sang songs praising good courageous actions, they sang songs that abused and mocked people who did wrong. These wandering singers and story-tellers were responsible for sustaining the culture and its customs; they were the real creators of the minds and souls of the people.

The bardic orders of the Celts and Teutons stretch back to the roots of early Indo-Germanic culture of Asia, to the period of the Indian Veda. In India traces have remained until today. Mircéa Eliade accordingly says of the ancient singers of myth and their declamation of particularly intimate holy texts: '... they can only be recited during the sacred seasons, in the bush and at night, or around the fire before or after the rituals, etc.'[6]

The custom of sitting in a circle around the fire to receive the message of the word and the song is described in the nineteenth century by the bards of Finland. The Finn, Dr Elias Lönnrot (1802–1884), the collector of the *Kalevala* texts, experienced this in his lifetime:

> As the sun set the people sat down in a circle on the hill around a fire and listened to the singing of two bards. (The *Kalevala* singers always appeared in pairs.) In the evening the old singer and his younger companion sat facing each other near the fire. They pressed their knees against each other and held hands, entwining their fingers, then they began to sway rhythmically. The old bard sang and the young one repeated like an echo and in this way the old songs often rang out all through the summer night:

Dearest friend, and much-loved brother,
Best beloved of all companions,
Come and let us sing together,
Let us now begin our converse,

...

Let us clasp our hands together,
Let us interlock our fingers;
Let us sing a cheerful measure,

(Kalevala, Runo I, ll.11ff)

The Finnish research into the last bardic survivals gives some idea of the range of bardic song culture in the north. In 1835 Lönnrot alone published no less than 12,078 verses in thirty-two songs. This work of collection was carried on by the successful student Europaeus, who himself recorded 2,800 songs. As a result the final edition of the *Kalevala* (1849) contained 22,795 verses. Enthusiasm for collecting followed in the Finnish Literary Society and the scholars it supported produced 45,000 songs for Finland, and as many as 70,000 for Estonia. For the most part these are contained in the *Kalevala* studies of Kaarle Krohn.[11] Clearly the Nordic bards were once a powerful force in sustaining a culture. In many European countries it was restricted at an early date by the Christian Church or died out completely with the coming of the new civilization.

As already shown, Ireland had bardic schools in pre-Christian times, as well as in the early Christian period. G. Murphy mentions about the later period that the metrical treatises of the tenth century specified the metres and the heroic literature which had to be studied each year in a twelve year course of study.[7]

The idea was that a man called to leadership should be able to hear 'the music of silence in his heart'. It was held that a good bard should have the heart of a bird when a child and therefore his own 'heart will palpitate for ever.'[8]

It is peculiar to Ireland that the pre-Christian, Celtic bardic schools continued into the Christian period, and that the ancient lays of the gods and heroes of mythology continued to be heard, with Christian texts enriching the forms of ancient tradition. J. Pokorny has recorded a lyrical poem emanating from Christian times (eighth century) about an island of the blessed in the distant West where Manannán, the heathen god of the sea, rises:[9]

Emhain
I know an island in the distant west
Round which the gleaming sea horses play
And swim towards the island's white sea shore
Raising aloft four columns that shine bright ...

There is no complaint and no betrayal
In those rich familiar fields;
No harsh sound jars upon the ear
Sweet music is all that can be heard ...

Across the surface of the sea gold chariots roll
Towards the sun as the high tide rises ...

A fair-haired man (who is Manannán)
Is seen in the rays of the rising sun,
Before him the land glows in the bright light
Towards which he drives over the expanse of sea ...

Here is another song from the *Book of Ballymote* into which, as in the song 'Emhain', no Christian element has yet penetrated. It sings of the bard's nature-spirituality and his ability to penetrate and lie in the objects and creatures of the world. The roots of the song must be very old.[10]

This is the song of the bard Taliesin, a pupil of Merlin
I am the wind that blows upon the sea
I am the ocean wave;
I am the murmur of the surges;
I am seven battalions;
I am a strong bull;
I am an eagle on a rock;
I am a ray of the sun;
I am the most beautiful of herbs;
I am a courageous wild boar;
I am a salmon in the water;
I am a lake upon the plain;
I am a cunning artist;
I am a gigantic, sword-wielding champion;
I can shift my shape like a god.

Ancient Irish bards in new Celtic collections

The revival of bardic poetry with Ossian which conquered and enraptured James Macpherson in the eighteenth century had the virtue of arousing the enthusiasm of collectors and poets of sagas, legends, myths, songs and epics at a time when the last remnants of folk tradition were dying. The romantic period that followed was particularly sensitive to its influence. A great deal was rescued from oblivion and carried forward into the twentieth century. This folk tradition enables us today to build vital bridges into mythic times from its recollections and the images conveyed by its words. We have already mentioned the formation of an Irish Ossianic Society which published ancient bardic texts in the middle of the nineteenth century. In addition many collections appeared in connection with the Irish literary movement which was led by W.B. Yeats (1865–1939). In his early poems in particular he included a great deal of Celtic tradition. Alexander Carmichael (1832–1912) researched devotedly the Celtic texts in the Hebrides and in the Highlands. He was one of those engaged in this research who had emotional ties with the Gaelic-speaking population. His work, part of which was published by his daughter and grandson after his death, displays in several volumes profound insight into the spiritual characteristics of these Celtic people and of their ancient tradition.

The Celtic scholar Ella Young (1867–1956) learnt the art of story-telling in Ireland directly from the story-tellers, the sennachies. She lived and made her collection for twenty years among the Gaelic-speaking people of West Ireland and the Aran Islands:

> The stories were told me in Gaelic at times, at times in English. I heard them in cottages by turf fires, I heard them in brown-sailed fishing boats and on rocky hillsides. They are mixed in my mind with sunshine and sweet air and wide empty spaces: with lakes in Donegal, where faery horses are said to hide, with pools in Connemara where crested serpents, called Piasts, lift their heads, and with glittering inlets of the sea and mountains in Kerry. [11]

At the beginning of the twentieth century the 144 Irish legends and tales of an anonymous new Celtic bard, Mary L, were written down. She told them to a German student of Gaelic and they followed the oral tradition. She lived in them with complete identification. Martin Löpelmann published them with the title *Erinn*.

Padraic Colum describes the way in which the wealth of the sennachies' stories survives:

> ... The storyteller seated on a roughly made chair on a clay floor did not look unusually intelligent or sensitive. He certainly did not look histrionic. What was in his face showed that he was ready to respond to and make articulate the rhythm of the night. He was a storyteller because he was attuned to this rhythm and had in his memory the often repeated incidents that would fit it ... These notions were in the present writer's mind once upon a time when he sat in a cottage where the tradition of storytelling was still in being.
>
> A rhythm that was compulsive, fitted to daily tasks, waned, and a rhythm that was acquiescent, fitted to wishes, took its place. But when the distinc-

tion between day and night could be passed over as it could be in towns and in modern houses the change of rhythm that came with the passing of day into night ceased to be marked. This happened when light was prolonged until it was time to turn to sleep.

From 1923 to 1931 James Delagrey was still able to write down some two hundred folk tales dictated by a seventy-year-old fisherman and peasant who could neither read nor write. And until the 1950s Anna McLoon (Celtic Nic Luain) sang Gaelic songs and recited stories for weeks on end to an Irish student of folklore. These were contained in her phenomenal memory.[12]

That the order of bards was not without opposition in its day is shown by the sixth century stories of a battle of bards, which provide interesting insights into the development of the post-Christian bards. The tradition is contained in the Amra of St Columba.[13] Aed mac Ainmire was at this time King of Ireland. He summoned the most important men of Ireland and Scotland to an assembly at Drumceat (c. 575). He had founded a spiritual centre on Iona, from which Christianity was brought into Scotland. At this time Scotland was a tributary kingdom of Ireland. Columcille used his influence with the King of Ireland, who granted complete independence to the kingdom of Scotland. This helped the Christian mission of the Irish to Scotland. Then, however, the important dispute concerning the Irish bards was discussed. Originally the bards had enjoyed high esteem, but this had been undermined by a loosening of discipline, and they were not always well received. As hundreds of bards (about 1200) were moving around the country, and everywhere enjoying the ancient custom of free hospitality, abuses sometimes occurred. Influential people wanted to deal with this state of affairs by dissolving the ancient order of bards. Columcille intervened at this point. He persuaded the assembly that the undisciplined wandering about should be reformed by establishing bardic schools in settled centres, as had been done in previous times. Only in this way could the all-important role of the bards, that of preserving the soul of the folk, be fulfilled. This proposal was accepted. The status of bards as a result was confined to those appointed and to these were entrusted dwellings and land for the support of teachers and pupils. By this measure an ancient Celtic institution was once more preserved into Christian times and actually saved by one of the leading figures of old Irish Christianity.

Despite Viking incursions and despite the influence of a later Roman Church that had little understanding of 'heathen customs' many reminders of bardic culture survived until the beginning of the twentieth century in Celtic districts of Ireland and Scotland.

The Scottish writer William Sharp (1855–1905) better known by his pseudonym Fiona Macleod, describes in *Winged Destiny* how as a boy he wandered

around among the Gaelic-speaking inhabitants of the Hebrides. He describes a fisherman who every morning on rising went to the seashore and there deferentially
took his hat in hand and spoke his prayers and the runes into the breaking waves.
This fisherman once gave him this explanation: 'Every morning like this I take off
my hat to the beauty of the world.' And on another occasion: 'Fire is God's touch ...
and the light is God Himself, and water is the mother of life.'[14]

The work of Alexander Carmichael (1832–1912) makes clear the special part
played by the Highlands and Islands of Scotland in the preservation of the
bardic tradition. He was born on the Island of Lismore, and he was, like William
Sharp (Fiona Macleod), a wandering collector, full of devoted enthusiasm. With
great effort and despite indescribable difficulties he went on collecting for
years. He had the kind of unpretentious and willing personality to which works
handed down in a private tradition were confidently entrusted. Carmichael did
not always note down from whom he had received certain texts and where he
had found them. For him they were all components of a great Celtic tradition,
which had developed into a Christian one. Carmichael interprets this derivation
perceptively.

> It is the product of far-away thinking come down on the long stream of
> time. Who the thinkers and whence the stream, who can tell? Some of the
> hymns may have been composed within the cloistered cells of Derry and
> Iona, and some of the incantations among the cromlechs of Stonehenge
> and the standing stones of Callarnis. These poems were composed by the
> learned, but they have not come down through the learned, but through the
> unlearned.[15]

Dr Kenneth MacLeod relates an experience of Carmichael which reveals what these
traditional texts meant to simple island people.

> One evening, a venerable Islesman, carried out of himself for the time
> being, allowed Dr Carmichael to take down from him a singularly beautiful
> 'going to sleep' rune; early next morning, the reciter travelled twenty-six
> miles to exact a pledge that his 'little prayer' should never be allowed to
> appear in print. 'Think ye,' said the old man, 'if I slept a wink last night for
> thinking of what I had given away. Proud indeed shall I be if it give pleasure
> to yourself, but I should not like cold eyes to read it in a book.' In the
> writer's presence, the manuscript was handed over to the reciter to be
> burnt there and then.[16]

Carmichael did receive a rune for sleeping from another Gael, and he printed
it:

Repose
Thou Being of marvels,
Shield me with might,
Thou Being of statues
    And of stars.

Compass me this night,
Both soul and body,
Compass me this night
    And on every night.

Compass me aright
Between earth and sky,
Between the mystery of Thy laws
    And mine eye of blindness;

Both that which mine eye sees
And that which it reads not;
Both that which is clear
    And is not clear to my devotion.[17]

Like Fiona Macleod, Alexander Carmichael met old people from the Hebrides who used to make their way through lonely places, often walking for miles every day, in order to blend their own voices with the sounds of the waves, and the surf, and all the elements. Ann MacDonald of Lochaber supplied him with one of these hymns, which many people declaimed like a chant:

Rune before prayer
I am bending my knee
In the eye of the Father who created me,
In the eye of the Son who purchased me,
In the eye of the Spirit who cleansed me,
    In friendship and affection.
Through Thine own Anointed One, O God,
Bestow upon us fulness in our need,
    Love towards God,
    The affection of God,
    The smile of God,
    The wisdom of God,
    The grace of God,
    The fear of God,

> And the will of God
> To do on the world the Three,
> As angels and saints
> Do in heaven;
>> Each shade and light,
>> Each day and night,
>> Each time in kindness,
>> Give Thou us Thy Spirit.[18]

On Lismore John Stewart gave Carmichael a fragment, in which we can perceive the Celtic intermingling of nature and the spiritual, which is a characteristic of 'Celtic' Christianity:

> *Fragment*
> As it was,
> As it is,
> As it shall be
> Evermore,
> O Thou Triune
> Of grace!
> With the ebb
> With the flow,
> O Thou Triune
> Of grace!
> With the ebb
> With the flow.[19]

The earth and its elements, which in the pre-Christian Celtic vision of the world was one with the world of the gods, now appear united with the Christian Mystery.[26]

> *From a Christmas Carol*
> This night is the eve of the great Nativity,
> Born is the Son of Mary the Virgin,
> The soles of His feet have reached the earth,
> The Son of glory down from on high,
> Heaven and earth glowed to him,
> ...
> The mountains glowed to Him, the plains glowed to Him,
> The voice of the waves with the song of the strand,
> Announcing to us that Christ is born ... [20]

When we recall megalithic and Celtic sun worship we are not surprised that the sun is brought into the Christian mystery as a material symbol of God. The sun, which achieves a 'resurrection' every morning, has to be linked as the sun of the Easter Morning resurrection mystery:

Easter Sunday
The people say that the sun dances on this day in joy for a risen Saviour.

Old Barbara Macphie at Dreimsdale saw this once, but only once, during her long life. And the good woman, of high natural intelligence, described in poetic language and with religious fervour what she saw or believed she saw from the summit of Benmore:

'The glorious gold-bright sun was after rising on the crests of the great hills, and it was changing colour — green, purple, red, blood-red, white, intense-white, and gold-white, like the glory of the God of the elements to the children of men. It was dancing up and down in exultation at the joyous resurrection of the beloved Savour of victory.

'To be thus privileged, a person must ascend to the top of the highest hill before sunrise, and believe that the God who makes the small blade of grass to grow is the same God who makes the large, massive sun to move.'[21]

Christ himself in Old Irish Christianity is the Logos, which is embodied in the earth and which gleaming like the sun illuminates the darkness. He is the 'inner, spiritual sun' of the earth.

> A time ere came the Son of God,
>   The earth was a black morass,
> Without star, without sun, without moon,
>   Without body, without heart, without form.
>
> Illumined plains, illumined hills,
>   Illumined the great green sea,
> Illumined the whole globe together,
>   When the Son of God came to earth.[22]

What had been the fire ritual in megalithic and Celtic times found in Christian times a metamorphosis into the lighting of the Easter Fire. In Kildare, for example, the Easter Fire was kept alight by maidens until the following Good Friday, when it was extinguished. But it was lit again on Easter Day. Formerly fire was the symbol of the cosmic light, ('contact with God'), now it was the medium of connection with the Divine world, with the Christ, symbol of love's power to warm.

Blessing of the Kindling
I will kindle my fire this morning
In presence of the holy angels of heaven,
In presence of Ariel of the loveliest form,
In presence of Uriel of the myriad charms,
Without malice, without jealousy, without envy,
Without fear, without terror of any one under the sun,
But the Holy Son of God to shield me,
  Without malice, without jealousy, without envy,
  Without fear, without terror of any one under the sun,
  But the Holy Son of God to shield me.

God, kindle Thou in my heart within
A flame of love to my neighbour,
To my foe, to my friend, to my kindred all,
To the brave, to the knave, to the thrall,
O Son of the loveliest Mary,
From the lowliest thing that liveth,
To the Name that is highest of all.[23]

Just as now in humankind the sun appears in its spiritual manifestation, which Christ had brought to the earth — on almost all old Irish crosses Christ is placed in the centre of the sun circle — so the moon is considered to be a 'guide for the soul.' In an interesting hymn it is linked with the Virgin. This derives from Celtic star-worship.

The New Moon
She of my love is the new moon,
      The King of all creatures blessing her;
...
Be her guidance on land
      With all beset ones;
Be her guidance on the sea
      With all distressed ones.

May the moon of moons
      Be coming through thick clouds
On me and on every mortal
      Who is coming through affliction

> May the virgin of my love
> > Be coming through dense dark clouds
> To me and to each one
> > Who is in tribulation. [24]

The fact that the figure of Archangel Michael was particularly close to the warring Celts can be seen in many hymns. They form a kind of literary culmination of the phrase of absorbing Christian content into the Celtic world.

> *Michael Militant*
> O Michael Militant,
> Thou king of the angels,
> Shield thy people
> With the power of thy sword,
> Shield thy people
> With the power of thy sword.
>
> Spread thy wing
> Over sea and land,
> East and west,
> And shield us from the foe,
> East and west,
> And shield us from the foe.
>
> Brighten thy feast
> From heaven above;
> Be with us in the pilgrimage
> And in the twistings of the fight;
> Be with us in the pilgrimage
> And in the twistings of the fight ...[25]

Janet MacIosaig, a crofter's wife on South Uist, gave Carmichael the following Hymn to Michael, in which the influence of the Archangel reaches the everyday troubles and cares of a peasant about his cottage and his farm.

> *Michael the Victorious*
> Thou Michael the victorious,
> I make my circuit under thy shield,
> Thou Michael of the white steed,
> And of the bright brilliant blades,
> Conqueror of the dragon,

Be thou at my back,
Thou ranger of the heavens,
Thou warrior of the King of all,
    O Michael the victorious,
    My pride and my guide,
    O Michael the victorious,
    Thy glory of mine eye.

I make my circuit
In the fellowship of my saint,
On the machair, on the meadow,
On the cold heathery hill;
Though I should travel ocean
And the hard globe of the world
No harm can e'er befall me
'Neath the shelter of thy shield;
    O Michael the victorious,
    Jewel of my heart,
    O Michael the victorious,
    God's shepherd thou art.

Be the sacred Three of Glory
Aye at peace with me,
With my horses, with my cattle,
With my woolly sheep in flocks.
With the crops growing in the field
Or ripening in the sheaf,
On the machair, on the moor,
In cole, in heap, or stack.
    Every thing on high or low,
    Every furnishing and flock,
    Belong to the holy Triune of glory,
    And to Michael the victorious. [26]

7. The Hymns of Old Irish Christianity

The numerous attacks by Vikings and Danes after 795 resulted in all the old Irish monasteries being overrun and ransacked one after another. Many of them were pillaged and completely destroyed. A small, outwardly almost intact remnant, is the site of the monastery on the rocky island Skellig Michael, which is in the Atlantic and difficult to approach. The island has vivid examples of primitive stone buildings, which provided rough shelter for the monks. Only intense spiritual experience could make such solitude bearable.

The ceaseless destruction led to nearly all manuscripts of the early Christian period in Ireland being lost. What had been preserved in the Continental monasteries was considerably reduced by the purges of Romanization. Very often undesirable parchment was reused as the material for new volumes. These factors resulted in a few fragments being preserved in liturgical texts which reached the Continent by way of England. Versions of the Gospels have been preserved in such outstanding books as the Book of Durrow and the Book of Kells. Hidden in the little town of Kells the latter book even survived the terrible period of Cromwell's regime, when the mere presence of a book in an Irishman's house was punished with death.

The hymns and liturgies

The Mass was not originally (before 700) celebrated in its Roman Catholic form. Communion was indeed the centre of the Irish ritual, embedded in its own richly varied liturgy. Adamnan reports an afternoon liturgical service, in which the hands and feet of the participants were washed.[1]

The *Antiphony of Bangor* (Ambrosian Library, Milan) is among the surviving treasures from the time before the eighth century, a collection of hymns and prayers from the year 680. An even older source is the 'Turin Fragment' from the monastery at Bobbio.[2] They illustrate the peculiar harmony of Celtic nature-worship with Christian spirituality, at the same time echoing the hymns of the Old Testament and Psalms in praise of the creation.

> As already in the darkness the cock-crow
> Heralds the approaching light of day
> So in the morning hour the song of Christians
> Who still are in the dark of earthly life
> Proclaim the future life, God's greatness
> And the rule of Christ.

Figure 51. Stone in the shape of a human, with engraved cross. Skellig Michael.

Benediction

May the divine work of creation be praised with hymns
Through all the ages!
May the sky of the Lord be praised!
Praised be the angels of the Lord,
Praised be the waters above the skies,
Praised be the heavenly powers,
Praised be the sun and moon,
Praised be the divine stars,
Praised be the rain and the dew,
Praised be all spirits,
Praised be the nights and the days,
Praised be darkness and light,
Praised be cold and heat,
Praised be frost and snow,
Praised be the lightning and the clouds,
Praised be the mountains and the hills,
Praised be all creatures born on earth,
Praised be the seas and the rivers,
Praised be the fountains and springs of water,
Praised be all creatures that loom in the water,
Praised be the fowls of the air,
Praised be the animals and all beasts of burden,
Praised be the people of Israel,
Praised be the sons of men,
Praised be the saints,
Praised be all servants,
Praised be the spirits and souls of the just,
Praised be all godly and humble hearts,
Praised be Ananias and Azarias, Misael.
The only all-powerful God,
We praise thy righteousness!
Thou who has freed the three youths from the fire
And has saved us from death
With thy pure compassion
Have mercy on us!
Praise be to thee from all things!

These themes of creation and praise are followed by texts dealing with Christmas, the magi and Christ's Passion.

A characteristic of the Old Irish Christianity with its Celtic myths is its deeply-felt appreciation of nature, indeed its enthusiasm for nature. It was clear to these 'Celtic' Christians that the spirit holds sway in the earthly and in human beings just as much as in the cosmos. Nature as a creation of the Logos is visible evidence of all-powerful, fatherly creative power. There is no strict separation into the here below (the physical world) and a hereafter (the spiritual world). The 'Benediction' demonstrates the mythic single dimensional character of creation, where hierarchies, stars, nature and her components, human beings and creatures are part of a single, immense whole, to which religious man turns and hymns his gratitude. This untheological, nature-monism is a Celtic inheritance, and in Northern Europe, especially among the Teutons, it prepares the way for the ready acceptance of Irish Christianity. It was one of the conditions favouring the Old Irish Christian missionaries that they could make contact with this nature spirituality imbued with divinities. They added to this the Christ-event as a new earthly mystery and taught that it was to be understood as a manifestation of the sun Logos incarnated in the earth and in mankind.

The examination of crosses with a sculptured figure will show that there was a belief in an apocalyptic teleologic human development: original sin (the Fall of man), incarnation of Christ in the Baptism, Passion and Resurrection. From this follows the release from sin as a possible transformation and elevation of humanity by means of striving through Way (imitation), Truth (wisdom), Life (in love for your neighbour and all creatures). Theologically and philosophically Pelagius had already advocated this in the year 400.

Whenever we come upon hymns, rituals and works of art in the period *before* Romanization in Ireland we find affirmation of the possibility of an *individual* path to the Christ and Mystery. The affirmation of 'success through striving and effort' belongs to this evolutionary optimism.

Just as Roman Christianity turns to the crucifixion, to the aspect of human suffering on earth, to the Passion, in Old Irish Christianity is found above all the triumphant, resurrected Christ, like the sun at work on earth and among people. All early Irish representations of Christ on the stone crosses show him in the sun circle giving blessing and conquering death. It is clear that the Gospel of John is alive here. The Christian order of bards impressed this spirit on the hymns inside the monasteries. Here is a further example of this characteristic union of spiritual and nature images.

> *Litany of Creation*
> I entreat Thee by the tenth order* in the compact earth;
> I entreat laud-worthy Michael to help me against demons.
> Together with Michael I entreat Thee by land and sea unrestingly; I

---

* Humanity is seen as the tenth level of the hierarchy.

entreat Thee without contempt by every property of God the Father.

I entreat Thee, O Lord, by the suffering of Thy body white with fasting; I entreat Thee by the contemplative life,

I entreat Thee by the active life.

I entreat the company of heaven with Michael for my soul; I entreat the saints of the world to help me on earth.

I entreat the company of heaven and bright-armed Michael; I entreat Thee by the triad, wind and sun and moon.

I entreat Thee by water and the cruel air; I entreat Thee by fire, I entreat Thee by earth.

I entreat Thee by the trinity, the arched torrid (zone), I entreat Thee by the two temperate (zones). I entreat Thee by the two frigid (zones).

I entreat Thee by the compass of the tuneful firmament; I entreat every stately-branching order, the host of the bright stars.

...

I entreat Thee by Thy love, which is deeper than the ocean; I entreat Thine own self, O King of the fierce sun.

...

I entreat Thee by time with its clear divisions, I entreat Thee by the darkness, I entreat Thee by the light.

I entreat all the elements in heaven and earth, that the eternal sweetness may be granted to my soul.

Thy boundless pity, Thy might over battles, Thy gentleness to Thy debtors, O beloved speedy King (?)

To help me out of every conflict, by them I entreat Thee, O Father.

I entreat.[3]

As we are informed that in a number of old Ireland's larger monasteries groups of monks took turns in singing so that 'eternal song' resounded in the monastery chapel, we realize that a large number of similar hymns must once have been available. The Psalms of David in the Bible were also used. Then there were places where all through the short summer nights twenty-four psalms were sung and still more as autumn approached and yet more as darkness increased and from November 1 (Samhain) until the New Year thirty-six psalms were sung in the long nights. In this way the darkness of winter was countered by an increased number of hymns, with the object as it were, of equalling it spiritually, and controlling it.[4]

Among the oldest known hymns there is the following, which in some places hints at the protective mantra of a missionary. It is dated in the eighth century. It was later attributed to St Patrick.

Figure 52. The triumphal Christ. Detail of east side of Muiredach Cross at Monasterboice.

With powerful strength I raise myself today
And invoke the Trinity
With belief in the threefold nature
And affirmation of the unity
Of the creator of the universe.

...

I rise today
By virtue of Christ's birth and baptism.
Crucifixion of Christ, burial of Christ,
Resurrection and ascent into heaven,
Return and descent to the last judgment.
I rise today by virtue of the love of the cherubim,
Of the devotion of angels
Of the service of the archangels

...

I rise and worship
The powers of the heavens.
Light of the sun,
White gleam of the snow
The glow of fire
The speed of the lightning
The rushing of the wind
The depths of the sea
The firmness of the earth
The hardness of rocks

...

Christ be with me
Christ in front of me
Christ behind me
Christ be in me
Christ below me
Christ above me
Christ on my right hand
Christ on my left hand

...

Christ in my heart, that thinks of me
Christ in my mouth, that speaks of me
Christ in my eye, that looks at me
Christ in my ear, that listens to me.

I rise today with greater strength
And invoke the Trinity
Believing in the threefold nature
And affirming the unity
Of the Creator of the Universe.[5]

In this hymn the Johannine Logos concept is joined with the Pauline 'Christ in me' (John 1:1f) to form a meditation mantra. Christ appears here as a cosmic creative essence and at the same time as the inner force of the human 'I' which is to be sought. For the old Irish monk it was also a question of life pledged to the imitation of Christ aiming at Christ's incarnation in the depths of his being. In such a practice no mention is made of the Church as a mediator. Path to the Christian mystery is sought by an individual, although this too was practised in brotherly communities.

8. Monks and Monasteries

In the rise and growth of Old Irish Christianity little regard was paid, even at the outset, to external organizations. Total contemplation was the Christian path, the fusion of self with the spirit of nature, humanity and earth now enriched by the Christ mystery. An ecclesiastical mentality was completely lacking. Reports are of solitary hermits, striving to attain 'purification' in isolation, in order to become better instruments for spiritual research. Small fraternities often formed around certain of these eremites. Some of these original formations developed into larger monastic settlements. On the West Coast in particular there is a chain of small islands on which anchorites (hermits) or a small community led their ascetic lives, surrounded by the surge of the sea.

The monks often lived together in groups of seven or twelve, as a 'community of the Lord's table,' who celebrated communion in a daily meal. So it was with a group of twelve companions that Columbanus set out for the Continent in the sixth century. Kilian carried out his missionary work in Thuringia with a band of twelve. In these monastic settlements married couples and families lived as well as the monks as late as the seventh century, sharing in the pursuits of a monastic life. The Old Irish monasteries did not have celibacy enforced by rule; there was rather a voluntary celibacy.

There existed in freedom the most varied spiritual and social forms, both those loosely connected and those closely involved with a religious centre. The monastic orders frequently replaced the leagues of warriors. Gradually certain rules developed among the larger communities. In the earlier period these remained oral agreements and only later were they written down here and there. In their early

Figure 53.

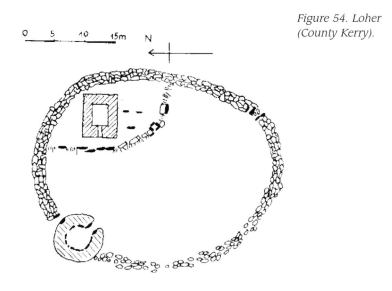

*Figure 54. Loher
(County Kerry).*

stages they had a metrical poetic form. They are mentioned in connection with Albeus (Ailbhe) of Emly (died *c.* AD 540) and Kieran of Clonmacnoise (died *c.* AD 549).[1] Self-training in the Christian virtues was recommended, and advice given on living together in a spirit of brotherhood. The small and the very small communities adopted the Gospel saying: 'Where two or three are gathered in my name, there am I in the midst of them' (Matt.18:20).

Individual sites from this early period have been preserved, such as the settlement at Duvillaun More (County Mayo) and Loher (County Kerry). The huts they lived in and the oratory (chapel) were often made of wood, and so have completely disappeared.

Skellig Michael, the island monastery in the Atlantic

Twelve kilometres (seven and a half miles) south-west from the Irish coast a rocky island rises up in the Atlantic and climbs up to a height of 210 metres (700 feet) above the sea. Shaped like a pyramid it rears up out of the deep blue water. It is said that in pre-Christian times it was already inhabited by Druids. The best-preserved remains of a monastery of the early period of Irish Christianity can be found there today. This was dedicated to the Archangel Michael. The foundation date of the monastery is not known.

Stone buildings stand above a protecting wall. A steep, primitive stone stairway with over 500 steps and a rocky path lead up to the site of the monastery at the top. Even in moderate seas it is impossible to land on the rocks. In a storm the spray is said to fly over the ridge. One can imagine that during winter storms the monks

Figure 55. Skellig Michael Monastery from the air.

Figure 56. Beehive cells.

were unable to undertake the dangerous and difficult voyage to the coast in their coracles (leather boats). The monastery itself had two oratories and a number of cells shaped like beehives, built of stone slabs. There was living accommodation for between twenty and thirty brothers. The small cemetery whose monument was a cross in human form received the brothers who had died. Here and there retaining walls have been built on the steep rocky slope to keep the sparse earth in the small, terraced gardens. A few goats could be kept here, and deposits of peat supplied a little fuel for heating. In these eyries the monks led their ascetic lives for centuries, free from any disturbing external influences, devoting themselves entirely to their voluntarily chosen path of purification and meditation. Anyone who has stood for any length of time on Skellig Michael and has looked down from its height on the deep blue of the sea and heard the distant thunder of the surf will understand that the primitive landscape provided an ideal environment for the pursuit of a holy life in the contemplation of the interplay of wind and clouds, of the waves of the ocean and the light throughout the passage of the days and years.

This place was called Michael's Rock (Sceilg Mhichíl) and was dedicated to the Archangel Michael, the Dragon Fighter, as a kind of Michael's Mount. With this situation it occupied a unique position among the early Irish monastic settlements. At the beginning of the ninth century it too was plundered by the Vikings. We do no know if the monks were able to escape or whether they were killed. Subsequently there came into existence near Bolus Head on the coast opposite a new monastery which had the name Ballinskelligs (Sanctuary of the Rock), where it is said surviving monks continued to live their communal life. The island monastery has remained empty ever since that time.

Other monasteries

In the Book of Mulling (Trinity College, Dublin) there is an unusual plan of the ideal layout of a monastery. This was perhaps a guide for a number of vanished monasteries. A remarkable feature of this guide is that the outline of the plan is based on the Old Irish sun cross (Figure 60).

The monastery buildings are to be imagined as being inside the circle of the wall. Outside the wall at the four cardinal points of the compass stand the tall crosses of the evangelists, lines radiating from them divide the circle into quadrants. At the end of the diagonals are the modest crosses of the four great prophets of the Old Covenant, Isaiah, Jeremiah, Ezekiel and Daniel. In the circle itself is the cross of the Holy Spirit, separating the monastery from the world, as it were, with the spiritual emblem of the sun ring. Inside the ring is the cross of the angels and that of Christ and the Apostles. An inscription on Oengus-Céli-Dé, which has come down to us, interprets the marking-off of the site of a monastery by a circle.

Figure 57. Part of the monastic stairway.   *Figure 58. The Wailing Woman stone.*

Figure 59. View from the South Peak hermitage out across Little Skellig.

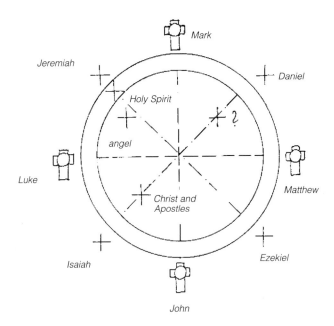

Figure 60.

> In Disert Bethech did he live
> He who was visited by a flight of angels
> In this pious monastery, surrounded by the circle of crosses
> He spent the best years of his life.[2]

The Irish stone crosses on the sites of monasteries had the purpose of marking out a 'spiritual place,' where people came together for prayer, for ritual and the Word. It is possible to imagine a particular kind of procession taking place in the course of the monastic routine. This would, for instance, lead the monks round the circle of the prophets. At the cross of each prophet they would listen to passages from their texts. They would then parade on to the crosses of the evangelists, where they would receive the new revelation.

A reconstruction of the monastery of Kells (Figure 61) hangs as a picture in the present day Church of Kells. It gives a clear picture of how an Irish 'monastic village' may have looked. It should be noticed that outlying settlements surround the central nucleus. They had closer or looser contact with the monastic life. Larger monastic settlements had an abbot who guided its religious and spiritual life. The vice-abbot was responsible for controlling discipline and the monastic rule (the realm of law). The butler (ceallóir), as steward of provisions, was entrusted with the

Figure 61. Reconstruction of the monastery of Kells.

care and conduct of the monastery's housekeeping. He saw to the food supply, which was almost entirely vegetarian, but with the welcome supplement of fish. Bees were kept not only for their honey but also for their wax, with which candles were made. He was also responsible for the care of guests and the poor.[3] Guests, who included travellers passing by, would be taken first of all to prayer in the chapel. Then a ritual washing of feet was carried out (following John 13:5ff) and only then were they conducted to the laden table. This reception was governed by the saying: 'Christ is our abbot and you are his guest.'

The abbot of a monastery had to decide the major problems, and he had to be obeyed completely. At his side was the 'council of the elders.'[4] In the monastery of Clonmacnoise this council lived in its own house. The elders were examples to and trainers of the novices.

The leading scribe had high rank, and passed the tradition of copying and illuminating manuscripts on to the other scribes.

Manual work was performed by monks allotted to this. But both abbot and bishop did not exempt themselves from manual work and at times ground corn, and worked in the garden and the fields.

There were nunneries, and some mixed monasteries. Brigid's (Bride's) monastery in Kildare was a mixed one, headed by an abbot and an abbess.

At first newly entered novices lived in a guest-house and stayed there until their commitment and aptitude had been tested, which could take up to three years. When they were accepted they received a new name and accepting this, they put aside their past. They often had to build their own cells, if no empty cell was available.

The habit of early Irish monks was white. Over this in cold weather they wore a woollen habit with a hood, and a coat as well when on a journey. The staff acquired great importance among itinerant monks (as it had earlier among the Druids). It was a symbol of the union with the divine which was being proclaimed on earth by the act of wandering. Mochoe's staff was called *in Etach* (the winged one) because in the legend it had come from heaven. Columbanus ordered that after his death his staff should be taken back to Gallus (550–645) (Figure 48).

The meals were deliberately kept as frugal as possible and in some monasteries the only meal each day was the evening meal. Bread was considered the most important food and was baked twice to make it keep longer. Periods of fast were carried out as exercises and could last as long as forty days after the example of Christ in the wilderness. There are some accounts which report that the monks held a stone in their mouths during a fast.

Inner peace was taught in periods of silence, during which communication by means of hand signals was permitted. In the larger monasteries prayer and meditation had to sustain an uninterrupted spiritual stream all through night and day. Continuity was ensured by shifts. It is said about individual prayer that the monk should from time to time perform a large number of knee-bending exercises in order to keep awake. Before the cross the praying monk stretched out his arms in the form of a cross and persisted in this position throughout a long prayer. Adamnán mentions a liturgical ceremony in which the washing of feet was carried out. The daily rite was communion, and until the eighth century this was accompanied by their own liturgy, and was not in the form of the Catholic Mass.

Art, language and scholarship in monastic culture

Until the sixth century, monastic culture must be considered a religious aspiration and endeavour which in material matters was undemanding and poor, and which indeed commended poverty as a virtue. There was, therefore, no 'art' as such. This only existed in the study of the Word and in religious ceremony. The traditional Celtic art of bronze jewellery and weapons went its own way and only later found contact and use in ecclesiastical and monastic utensils. In the seventh century there occurred a sudden and astonishing flowering of the art of lettering, of metal and enamel work as well as of stone carving. It accompanied the spread of missions on the Continent. The few surviving examples, such as the 'Book of Durrow,' and the Chalice of Ardagh (Figure 62) are evidence of craftsmanship. The forms and shapes are spirals and graded lines from pre-Christian time. These, too, enter Christian art quite intact. The graves of Vikings in Norway brought to light in particular metalwork of the eighth and ninth centuries.

Figure 62. The Chalice of Ardagh.

Among the early monastic schools those of Enda of Aran (late fifth century), of Finian of Clonard (founded in 520) and of Kieran of Clonmacnoise (founded in 548) are known. Many others have vanished. There are no records of the early period of monastic life. Pelagius spoke Greek and Latin and was master of a highly sophisticated philosophical language. He has a unique place in history as almost the sole early missionary from Ireland and he is evidence of the high level of early Irish monastic culture (see Chapter 11). J.F. Kenney reports: 'The poet shows a knowledge of the Greek and Hebrew letters and their use.'[5] In the sixth century Latin in Ireland was usually in the style of *Hisperica Famina*, which uses Hebrew words as well as Greek words.[6] It is reported of Abbot Mo-Sinu maccu Min of Bangor (died 610) that he had learnt how to calculate Easter 'from a Greek scholar.'

The Lord's Prayer in the 'Book of Armagh' (AD 807) is in Latin, but it is still written in Greek characters.[7] H. Zimmer considers that the style of Columban's works show that he knew Greek.

The three languages of Hebrew, Greek and Latin were reckoned 'holy languages.' They must have been cultivated before the eighth century in a number of monasteries, which means works in these three languages were known. After Romanization, that is to say after 700, only Latin, the language of the Roman

Church, was cultivated, although this change seems to have occurred much later in some monasteries. A later witness of this is the great John Scotus Erigena, (c. 810– c. 877) who translated some important Greek books (see Chapter 18). Macalister, writing on the legend of the Old Irish Ogham script, considers that the sequence of signs show that it was formed from the Greek alphabet.

It is very difficult to determine (in the absence of sources) what was taught in the monasteries that was not biblical. One or two hints are given by Irish monks who migrated to the Continent.

Virgilius of Salzburg (c. 700–784) still remained loyal to the tradition of Irish Christianity when Bishop of Salzburg in the period of Romanization. He was a thorn in the flesh of Pope Zacharias (died 752) and the fanatical Boniface (675–754). In nine letters to Boniface, Pope Zacharias complained that Virgilius thought that the Antipodes existed and that the sun and moon were underneath the earth as well as above. There is not another word surviving about Virgilius, which is no surprising as he was branded a heretic. His name was expunged from the list of bishops.[8] In 825 Dungal, from Bangor (County Down), was invited to the University of Pavia because of his great knowledge. A letter of his has been preserved which was written to Charlemagne in 810. In it he explains the double eclipse of the sun in 810 using Copernican ideas.

Dicuil (died 825), of the Irish monastic school at Clonmacnoise, wrote a work *Liber de Mensura Orbis Terrarum* (On measuring the earth). In it he mentioned the midnight sun in the north (Thule), with a description of the Nile which he had received from Brother Fidelis, who had made the pilgrimage to the Holy Land. He also wrote about astronomy in both prose and verse, which has not been published to this day.[9]

Unfortunately the proverbial Irish monastic erudition, which was so often mentioned by contemporaries in many different places, has not survived. The reasons for this are the destruction of documents in the periods of invasions which was followed by the heresy hunts and restrictions of the medieval Church, which destroyed such characteristic sources as the writings of Pelagius and Erigena on the grounds that they confused the spirit.

The monastic ideal

The large number of monasteries in their great period (sixth to ninth centuries) and the number of inmates show that a monastic mode of life was firmly founded on the national character of the island. The monasteries of Bangor, Clonfert and Clonard in their great period had each three thousand monks. Originally there were no differing orders and all acknowledged each other as brothers in Christ. Monasteries cultivated friendly relationships with each other so that monks form different monasteries met in joint communities for prayer.[10] The life of a hermit, though, was more highly esteemed than monastic life.

In the *Homilies of Cambra* (eighth century) three levels of martyrdom are introduced as conforming to the ideals of Irish monks. 'There are three ways in which a man can carry his cross — the white martyrdom, the green martyrdom and the red martyrdom.'[11]

The ideal of the first level, the white one, concerns the body to be cleansed, the 'bleached body,' the endurance of privation; detaching oneself from everything one loves, undertaking fasting and suffering 'in order to achieve the love of God.'

On the second level, the green one, purification is to be carried further into the realm of the soul as far as complete renunciation and absence of all desire. The aspirant examines retrospectively his previous life with its errors and sins. He repents, he atones (purgatory).

On the third and highest level, that of red martyrdom, he gains the level of a courageous missionary, who with fearless spirit is ready to go into the world and surrounded by persecution to give his blood for the kingdom of God, ready to suffer death for love of Christ and his kingdom.

The historian cannot help viewing with awe these anchorites and monks striving for centuries in isolation, who in spiritual union with the brotherhoods of the great monastic centres gave meaning to the name 'Island of Saints.' They created the spiritual foundation for the 'Irish missionaries.'

The churches

According to a number of accounts the commonest type of building in the early period was the wooden church. Bede (*c.* 673–735) mentioned such a church in Lindisfarne (Holy Island, England) and added that it 'was like the Irish churches, not built of stone but entirely of oak with a roof of reeds.'[12] As well as wooden churches there were stone churches in desolate barren regions of the west in particular, and on the islands. The earliest examples are the famous Oratory of Gallarus on Dingle Peninsula, Skellig Michael, Clonmacnoise and other places (see Figures 63 and 64). The basic plan of them all is a rectangle without any curve at the choir end and without any separation of the sanctuary from the congregation. The interior was dark and without any altar; sometimes there was a small window letting in light and facing the east. For prayer darkness was entered, or an interior faintly illuminated by wax candles. Only in the Romanizing period did the separation of the nave of the church (congregation) and the choir (the priest) take place. From the transitional period churches are found where the original east wall has been broken down and in its place a Roman apse built. There is an example at Kilmalkedar (County Kerry). There were very few large churches. Instead, where there was a demand, a number of small churches were built. 'To this day, in the more remote parts of Ireland, the men attend Mass outside the church-door in the open air — a polite gesture to the ladies, which dates from the times when church buildings were normally too small to hold the entire congregation.'[13]

Figure 63. Oratory of Gallarus on Dingle Peninsula.

Churches in certain districts had their own calendar and in particular their own festivals. The principle of individuality dominated here as well.[14] Baptism was generally done in running water or in the sea instead of dipping three times in still water.[15]

The custom of building stave churches continued in Norway for a long time. In Flå there still exist the foundations of a wooden church, which has no internal division. Such ground plans (from the seventh century) are also to be found on Lake Thun (Switzerland) where there is a legendary tradition of Irish missionary activity, in Spiez as well as in the nearby village of Faulensee.

The spiral and braided ornamentation of Norwegian stave churches still reveals an Irish origin as late as the twelfth and thirteenth centuries. They are similar to the interlacing lines of the Irish, such as are in the illustrated manuscripts of Ireland of the eighth and ninth centuries. They are indications of an Irish tradition in the conversion of Norway to Christianity, for which the historical evidence remains in darkness (see p.119ff).

The round towers

It is as much of a puzzle to determine when the first round towers were built as it is to trace their origin. Nowadays they are thought of as typically Irish as there

Figure 64. Tower of Glendalough (County Wicklow).

Figure 65. St Kevin's Kitchen, Glendalough (County Wicklow)

is nothing like them in Europe. Their use as simple refuge towers was at the most of secondary importance. They erect a clearly visible standard of the vertical in the landscape, like the menhirs in the megalithic period, obelisks in Egypt and the spires of Gothic cathedrals. The character of a widespread countryside, an entire valley, can be influenced and inspired by a single one of these round towers. The earth becomes visibly connected with an 'above,' whether it is now called heaven or the divine. The round towers marked the sites of the spirit, where lofty aspirations were practised and lived. The monks and master builders who built the towers of Ardmore and Glendalough to a height of more than twenty metres must have been aware of the effect of verticals. At the very top there are always four slotted windows, placed at the four points of the compass. Several times each day at the hour for prayer the monks climbed up ladder steps and rang a handbell in all four directions, holding the handbell out of the aperture. In this way an 'acoustic cross' sounded across the countryside so that their neighbours and those working in the fields (the monks often took the host with them when working in the fields) could participate in the prayer. The round tower therefore rose up from a 'sacred centre' to announce and to warn. Here the hungry pilgrims and travellers found food, the thirsty drink and hospitality. They received spiritual strength as well as provisions for the journey. The round towers gave an assurance that could be seen from afar that here was a place where men strove to link heaven and earth.

9. From the Pre-Christian to the Christian Cross

Pre-Christian cross motifs

Mythic man experienced himself as part of the cosmos. The old cults strove to foster and maintain this unbroken religious integration of mankind in the cosmos. Offenders, people who fell out of the ordered system of the universal cross, were lashed to the cross. It was believed that they could be brought back into the 'ordered system of the cross' by suffering and death, that they could be 'installed' again and integrated into the morality of the cosmos. The cross indicated the direction of the human-divine.

Thousands of years before Christianity the symbol of the cross was a revered and sacred sign. Its appearance in connection with ritual cults was global in extent and was particularly widespread in Northern Europe. In the Bronze Age it made a significant appearance in the rock carvings of Tanum, Sweden, in particular as the sun with an inscribed cross on the ritual boat.[1]

The general meanings are:

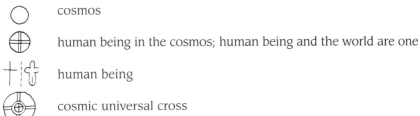

cosmos

human being in the cosmos; human being and the world are one

human being

cosmic universal cross

The universal cross and the sun cross are very often identical. The 'light of the world,' the sun, is the central spiritual source of every flourishing cosmic good. In the tumulus at Slieve na Caillighe (see p.32ff) we found an early form of the pre-Christian sun cross.

Figure 66. Rock carvings at Tanum, Sweden.

 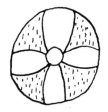 

Figure 67. Golden discs with motifs of sun crosses. Scythian.

In the National Museum at Bucharest pre-Christian sun cross motifs can be seen on Scythian gold discs. H. Kühn has examples to show that in America, on the other side of the Atlantic, the cross with the sun was one of the primitive symbols.[2]

The rock carvings of the sun at Hubelwängen near Zermatt, Switzerland, are very enlightening on the way in which the sun cross came into existence.[3]

 1. The rising sun in spring.

 2. The autumn and winter sun sinking down.

 3. The two joined, summer and winter suns at opposite poles.

 4. The four seasonal positions of the sun produce a cross: bottom, December 21; left, March 21; top, June 21; right, September 23.

 5. The sun with the four seasons engraved as a cross.

 6. Simplest form of the four positions of the sun as a simple cross.

Sun discs

In the National Museum at Dublin there are some plaquettes made of fine gold leaf from the pre-Christian megalithic age. They were found in pairs in graves and (according to J. Raftery of Dublin) were sewn on the clothes of a human being. In each case they were found on the breast bone of the skeleton and the two holes for the stitch are visible.

The gold discs have three symbolic themes which are worked with fine crafts-manship into the metal representing the sun: the outer ring, the aura of the sun chased as a circle, then the large cross of the sun in the circle with four sector corners in relief; finally in the centre the small cross of the star representing man, sustained by the surrounding circle.

The wearers of such symbolic discs were probably members of the religious leadership, and were priests or princes. The discs are evidence of the pre-Christian identity of light (sun) and cosmic order (cross). The wearers must have been ministers of this light-sun belief. They had the responsibility for leadership and for keeping mankind in this regime. Gold, the metal used here, is in harmony with the spiritual symbolic content.

Figure 68. Sun disc.

Figure 69. Sun disc of Linon, France.

The Christ sun disc of Linon

In the Cabinet des Medailles in Paris there is preserved a representation of Christ on a gold disc from the Puy-de-Dôme. Its date is about AD 650. This was the period when the Irish mission was actively spreading in France. In the centre of the disc is a face surrounded by an aureola with twelve divisions. The four quarters of the cross are marked on the inner circle with four squares; the other divisions are marked by rhombuses (lozenges) and a triangle. In the outer crossbeams alpha (A) is on the left and omega (ω) on the right; in one of the upper divisions there is an R (Rex) so that from the rays on the disc this can be deciphered: Christ, King of the Sun, of the Light, is the alpha and omega. The outer aura of the sun is decorated with plaited and spiral shapes. Whether there is Irish Celtic influence here or whether this particular symbolism reached France in some other way must remain an open question. The inner identity is clear.

In the megalithic age and in the Celtic epoch the sun was considered to be the divine centre of the cosmos. From the sun came the manifestation of creativity, the productive Logos. In Christianity from the very beginning these sun and Logos forces were united with the Christ who was incarnated on earth. And in this symbolism we find the Christ of early Irish Christianity and his cross is united with the symbol of the sun as is demonstrated with impressive abundance on the stone crosses.

Early Christian sun crosses

The transition from pre-Christian mythic feeling to Christianity took place in Ireland, as has been shown, in an unbroken, harmonious fashion. Old mythology was complemented and enriched around the Christian mystery. Accordingly Irish Christian symbolism in its early stages displays parallels with the pre-Christian symbolism and the development from it which is quite unique. Creativity flows into the traditional material and the old spirituality unites with the new. Witnesses to this transition are old ritual stones (menhirs and pillars) on to which Christian symbols had been carved. It is as though they were 'baptized' and made fit to receive the new signs.

An outstanding proof of this in stone is the pillar from Arraglen (Kerry) which once stood between the two peaks of Brandon Hill, (it is now in the National Museum in Dublin). It is often difficult to determine which of these ritual stones are pre-Christian and which should be given a later date. In the case of this stone pillar it may be a case of the stone which was already engraved in pre-Christian times, inasmuch as two swastikas are to be found on it, plainly visible despite weathering. Presumably the cross in a circle was engraved over them in the Christian period. The Ogham characters on the side only state that the originator was 'Ronan the priest, son of Comgall.' Between the forceful two 'Druid crosses' (sun swastikas) an arrow points toward the Christian cross, which brought the logos of the sun to earth. Clearly the intention is to say, 'the age of the Druid swastika has passed, fix your eyes on the Christ cross.'

This symbolically performed 'baptism' of the old ritual stone is met in many similar pillars and menhirs which had ritual importance in pre-Christian times. Two further examples are illustrated here. It could be supposed that these stones were pre-Christian ritual stones which had no symbols on them. They were given new emblems in the early Christian period. At the top there is the ring-sun-cross. From it forces flow symmetrically down through the stone, with spirals drawing everything through their arteries of light, just as human beings are to be revived into new life by the forces of Christianity.

It might also be thought that stones like those at Reask (County Kerry) and Inishkea (County Mayo) were first erected in Christian times. Their message remains the same: making visible the living Christian forces which have taken

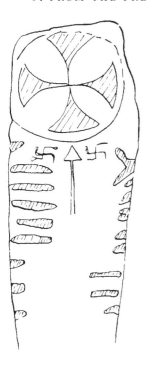

Figure 70. Stele of Arraglen
(County Kerry).

Figure 71. Stele of Reask,
Dingle Peninsula.

possession of the earth (the stone) and mankind. It seems senseless to speak of mere decorative ornaments in connection with such stones, as a purely aesthetic approach always does. The aesthetic approach rejects and passes over the deeper meaning of these documents in stone (see Figure 71).

The west side of the Kilree Cross (County Kilkenny) is most interesting from the point of view of sun symbolism. Here a religious idea is combined with an astronomical concept of the sun years (see Figure 72).

In the sun symbol and in the spiral it is possible to trace how pre-Christian symbols changed and developed into early Christian Irish symbols. In the centre of the cross in almost all early and late Irish stone crosses is Christ. In the oldest, which have the form of pillars, Christ is usually represented by the sun symbol. Here Christ is identified with the 'light of the world,' with the sun. Written texts from the early period in Ireland have unfortunately been lost. Nevertheless interesting evidence is provided in the *Confessions of Patrick*. In the surviving fragment Patrick contrasts Christ as the true sun with the old cult of the sun.[4] *'Nos autem qui credimus et ado-*

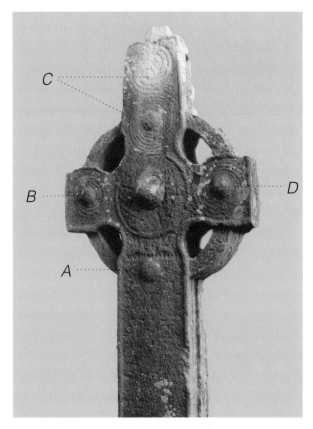

Figure 72. The west face of the cross at Kilree (County Tipperary).

A. The bare winter sun, below.
B. The spring sun unfolding in spirals.
C. The summer sun, expanding powerfully in the spiral and surging upwards.
D. Autumnal equinox with reversed spiral.

ramus solum verum Christum. (But we believe and worship the true sun, Christ, who will never set.)'

This is echoed by a surviving hymn in the Celtic tradition: 'Illumined the whole globe together,/When the Son of God came to earth.'[5]

There are parallel texts in early Southern Christianity and above all in the Eastern Church: Christ as the 'King of Heaven ... the ascending sun who shines also for the dead and mortals on the earth. As the true Helios he climbed the heights of heaven.'[6]

With Firmicus Maternus (died after 360) salvation is 'only in the Easter mystery of Christ, who as the sun illuminated the world below and then resplendent rose again on Easter Day.'[7] Similar ideas have already been mentioned (see p.78ff).

This early Christian evidence shows clearly why in early Irish Christianity the old sun symbol is found in the centre of the cross. Where parchment is lacking, the stone crosses speak a clear language. In some cases the sun is emphasized, in others the cross; there can scarcely be said to be a straightforward development of themes. There are, however, certain types which are equal in value and which do

Figure 73. Basic types of early Christian crosses.

1. Kilaghtee (Donegal). The cross is contained in the sun disc.
2. St Kevin's Cross, Glendalough. The freely shaped cross carries the sun in it.
3. Aghowle (Wicklow). The sun disc dominates.
4. National Museum, Dublin. The sun in it.
3. Aghowle (Wicklow). The sun disc dominates.
4. National Museum, Dublin. The sun nucleus (Christ) is surrounded by the three sun year emblems, carried in the cross.
5. Nurney (Carlow). Here the cross predominates with the sun nucleus (Christ) centre. The sun disc retreats.
6. Eustace East, Kildare. Another variation of penetration of sun disc and cross.
7. Reefert Church, Glendalough. The sun disc is formed as an unbroken ring.
8. East side of Kilree (Kilkenny). Sun disc with Christ-centre inside, sun aura ring outside carried by a dominating cross.
9. Southern Cross, Ahenny (Kilkenny). Cross with sun ring in harmonious balance. In the cross beams the signs of the Evangelists.

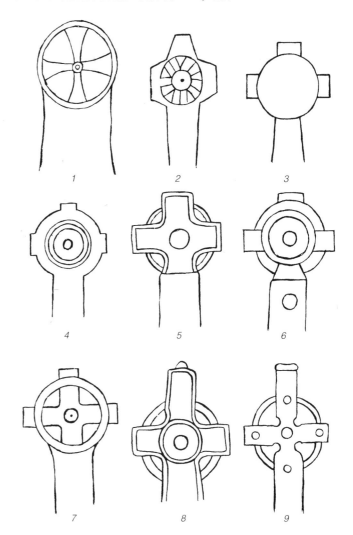

not permit any chronology to be formed. Nevertheless a definite metamorphosis of themes can be discerned in the duality of 'sun' and cross.

From near St Ninian's monastery Candida Casa (south-west Scotland) come wheel crosses (Whithorn Museum). These are really the sun disc crosses which were at one time engraved on pillars or shaped as a three-dimensional disc. By chiselling out the empty spaces a cross has been formed. The very old tombstone illustrated here points the strong 'bands' toward the earth. The sun disc rises freely above them (Figure 74).

On the Scottish island of Iona, a centre of Celtic Christianity in the sixth century, there stands a cross on which the Christ (centre) is surrounded by the circle of apostles. On the cross-shafts are the signs of the four evangelists. On the upright

Figure 74. Crosses at Whithorn (Galloway, Scotland), Iona (Scotland) and Duleek (County Meath).

beneath the cross, lozenges and other symbols of the sun have been engraved. (These cannot be seen in Figure 74.)

The east side of the north cross at Duleek (County Meath) displays in the sun centre seven markings which could be understood as planets and the dance around the sun. Seven was thought to be the number of planets (including sun and moon).

The lozenge (rhomboid) motif

The figures on Newgrange show that the lozenge too was an old sun symbol (and more rarely the square is tilted). It is not surprising therefore that this pre-Christian sun figure was adopted in the Irish stone crosses. In the eighth-century decorated cross at Moone (County Kildare) there is a lozenge on the west side immediately under the central sun swastika. The upper point of the lozenge projects into the area of the sun ring (Figure 75).

The west side of the cross at Dysert O'Dea (County Clare) has the sun lozenge in the centre surrounded by four other lozenges. In the lower part of the base the lozenge is repeated several times. It is a genuine 'rhombus cross.' The short cross-shafts still show at the side the pivot holes of the missing parts. Conceivably they were longer and surrounded by a stone ring.

In the 'Book of Kells' the lozenge occurs several times. On the second page of the Gospel according to St John there are four evangelists in the form of symbolic animals and angels. In their midst Christ is represented by the large sun lozenge. Two pages further on is the full-page portrait of John the Evangelist. He is holding the gospel, which begins with the words about the Logos. On the covering page is

Figure 75. The west face of the cross at Moone.
Figure 76. The west face of the cross at Dysert O'Dea (County Clare).

the large lozenge with an inscribed cross. There is a similar lozenge on the opening page of Luke's Gospel (Fig. 77).

These examples should be sufficient to demonstrate the transference of another pre-Christian figure, the lozenge, into Christian art.

Belief in the old gods, and the new revelation

The introduction of the old symbols and gods into the new Christian revelation was in conformity with the deeply-felt sense of spiritual continuity in old Irish Christianity. Heathen ritual stones were 'baptized,' old cult centres were linked with the new revelation. A remarkable parallel development of transference is found on the Baltic island of Gotland[8] which was Christianized by Irish missionaries.

As in the case of Norway the link between Gotland and Ireland is shown by a number of discoveries. A bay on Gotland is today still called Ireviken (Irish Bay). The

Figure 77 (opposite) . Book of Kells, The Gospel of Luke (fol, 188r).

Figure 78. Cross with sun-ring at Lau, Gotland

Figure 79. Stones with sun motifs. Gotland

beautifully decorated stones derive from pre-Christian Germanic culture, and certainly were part of the cult of the sun.

On Gotland, there are a number of 'Irish stone crosses' from the early Christian period. Following this and right into the thirteenth century a rich culture with wooden sun-ring crosses developed (Figure 78), which reach a height of 10 metres (33 feet).

In the 'Guta Saga,' an appendix to a Gotland book of laws of the fourteenth century, the chronicler reports the way in which the Gotlanders accepted Christianity: 'After the Gotlanders had become aware of the customs of Christian men they obeyed God's commandments and the teaching of the learned men. They accepted Christianity of their own free will, without compulsion, and so no one forced them into Christianity.'[9]

We see that the chronicler still mentions many centuries later the completely unconstrained acceptance of Christianity from the (Irish) missionaries. Roman Christianity used tougher methods.

On Gotland there were formerly Germanic family cult communities. Almost every farm had its sacrificial site. In the early Christian period these developed into a large number of small chapels and churches. The head of the family, just as he had formerly performed the sacrifice, now led the worship of the small community. Peripatetic priests came to the services from time to time.

Fragments of an eleventh century church have Irish twisted braid ornaments.[10] A rich braided ornamentation with Irish influence appears in the Norwegian stave churches.[11] The sun cross often appears here as a diagonal cross on balcony balustrades. In the stave church of Borgund the leaves of the Tree of Life sprout from the sun's symbol in the cross. Immediately underneath this a stag's head is still fastened today as a symbol of the powers of the sun. In a church built in the

Figure 80. One-eyed Odin. Capital in the stave church of Hegge, Norway.

Figure 81. Braid ornaments in Norwegian stave churches.

Figure 82. Vidar holding down the dragon with both hands, Mary and the child next to him. Capital in the Abbey of Payerne, Switzerland.

spirit of Celtic Christianity even the old gods were allowed to be present in the shapes of the pillars. The wooden Odin mask at Hegge is an echo of this (Figure 80). As the capital of a pillar he gazes with his one eye into the body of the church. He is the Nordic creator of the world, and for that reason is able to stand as a pillar in the hall of the Christian site where his mythic 'Word' transforms itself into the Christian Logos, into the Christian World. He must have made such a strong impression on the Germanic-Scandinavian world that Irish Christianity, which proclaimed the new god, rather than fight against and destroy the old gods, honoured them as forerunners of the new god's appearance.

It would be a study in itself to show how in all places where early Irish Christianity had an influence on the Continent, pre-Christian gods (up until the Romanesque period) were accepted into the body of the church.[12] For example the Vidar Column in the crypt of Freising Cathedral (Bavaria) was originally an Irish foundation of Corbinian (seventh century). The column shows the Germanic heroic god Vidar fighting the Fenris Wolf, the Nordic symbolic image for the opposing powers of darkness. This fight is portrayed in three episodes: in one he places his shoe on the dragon wolf, in the next he cuts its throat, finally he drives his sword into its heart.

There is a remarkable capital on his theme in the Romanesque Abbey of Payerne (Switzerland) near which at Romainmôtier in the Jura Irish Christianity was influential in an originally southern foundation. On the left is the Germanic hero god Vidar warding off the dragon with both hands; beside him is the peaceful figure of Mary holding the child in her lap. This relief is an expression of the twilight of the gods in which the old Nordic mythic world is vanishing. Vidar wards off the wolf dragon. This makes it possible for the new world to be introduced with the birth at Bethlehem — the old world of the gods goes under, the new mystery rises up. This is the view represented by the Vidar-Mary capital at Payerne, which was that of the Christian Irish missionaries and which here still permeates the Romanesque.

10. Main Themes of the Sun Crosses

On the reality of symbols: a digression

In the extensive literature on old Irish art and culture a certain attitude that seeks to simplify symbolism is frequently encountered. The cause may be that there is no authoritative interpretation of these phenomena or that all features of mythic religion are generally thrust aside from fear of being unable to handle them. In their place are irrelevant aesthetic consideration of themes and 'ornaments,' which are judged solely as decoration and considered as entirely external forms. There is talk of interesting effects of light and shade, of contrast, of 'animated surfaces.' In doing so the spiritual statement is completely neglected, a statement which is an indication of the fundamental relationship of pre-Christian religion with Christianity. The wheel cross is rejected as a symbol of the sun while at the same time it is maintained that it was originally a wooden cross whose cross-shafts were strengthened by wooden pieces rounding it off. The circle, it is asserted, arose round the cross for craft reasons and that this was simply carried over when stone crosses came to be made; and on them of course, it no longer had any function. Similarly the four buttons of the beams were simply the wooden nails which had secured the braces on the wooden cross carried over on to the stone cross. The 'sun centres' are explained by reference to metal crosses, on the centre of which a jewel was fastened. This practice, it is said, was imitated on the stone crosses.

A further hypothesis simply explains the crosses as the ornamentation of books carried out in stone. Such superficial treatment contradicts their deep religious spirit. In them and scarcely anywhere else the language of symbols gives insight into the transition, into the metamorphosis of pre-Christian religion into Christianity. The unbroken but metamorphosed survival of Celtic spirituality and intensity in Christianity gave Christianity after the first centuries in Ireland an impetus which spread it in the sixth century to Scotland, England and the Continent. Until late in the Middle Ages there was a spiritual fertilization coming from the north: *Ireland, Harbinger of the Middle Ages* is the title of a book by Ludwig Bieler.

If the pre-Christian symbols continued to function on Christian monuments, this does not imply any breakdown of Christianity. On the contrary, it demonstrates what unbroken development without the sword and without compulsion has achieved here in Ireland.

Twisted braid themes

On the early Christian crosses it is possible to show how the pre-Christian sun symbols affected its metamorphosis into the Christian period. Previously menhir,

Figure 83

1. Geometric 'mineral' shapes.
2. The vegetable kingdom: spiral and braid shapes; representations of leaves and blossoms.
3. Animal kingdom: dragon and snakelike twisted braids, with animal bodies and heads.
4. Twisted braids with human shapes and heads.

dolmen and cromlech united human beings, earth and cosmos in the ritual centre. In the sixth and seventh centuries the stone cross was erected in the open air to replace them. It proclaimed the new cult of the Logos that had come down to the earth and symbolized this with a sun centre in the earthly cross, adding the horizontal, which represented the earth, to the vertical (menhir). This expresses the entrance into the earth's gravity whose pull opposes the vertical. In Christian terms this means at the same time to turn to the surroundings, to the wealth of nature and to follow human beings as neighbours. The cross now becomes an expression of the field of forces embracing cosmos, earth and man, which finally leads to inescapable death. The cross is from the outset placed in the power of the sun, of the Logos. Sun centre and sun ring symbolize the forces of the Logos that have passed through the cross and which, overcoming death, lead to new life.

Another Christian symbol on the cross is provided by the twisted and interlaced braids. They appeared among the Hebridean Celts in the Iron and Bronze Ages. In Ireland, however, few have been found. The National Museum in Dublin has a few brooches and some scabards which are from the Celtic period and which have intertwined lines (Ballinderry, County Offaly, and Lisnacrogher, County Antrim among others). In England the outstanding discoveries of Sutton Hoo (Suffolk) are preserved, which were discovered in 1938. The untouched ship grave of a chief, with his weapons and jewellery from the sixth century, was found. The wealth of Celtic twisted braids in these discoveries is unique. They are preserved in the British Museum.[1]

Celtic twisted braids, whose origins are unchristian, also continue to exist in early Christian Irish crosses. A refinement of technique in stone carving was needed for these wonderful carvings to be chiselled into the stone. Simply to think of the intertwined braids as ornamental decoration leads away from their original meaning. In a wealth of varieties they were developed in the scriptoria of the monasteries and were embodied in the illumination of the Gospel manuscripts. After the eighth century their forms changed into virtuoso decorative ones, changed into merely aesthetic forms, as does happen to all symbolic forms, when the mythic religious experience deserts them.

Detailed investigation of the basic themes and the braid ornaments of early crosses and manuscripts reveals four groups of structures which relate to the four realms of nature:

1. Geometric, 'mineral' shapes.
2. The vegetable kingdom: spiral and braid shapes, representations of leaves and blossom.
3. Animal kingdom: dragon and snakelike twisted braids, with animal bodies and heads.
4. Twisted braids with human shapes and heads.

Figures 84 and 85. The east face of the North Cross of Ahenny (County Tipperary).

These four styles are often clearly set in panels next to each other, as for instance on the north cross at Ahenny. Low on the stem (east side) a geometric motif is found in three rows on top of each other. Next to them on the side of the column spiral plant shapes climb upwards. Above the geometric motif are three dragon heads entwined with each other in each of four swastika spirals held together by a fifth central swastika (Figures 84 and 85).

Above the leaves in the sphere of the sun ring an interwoven net emerges from the sun symbol and weaves through and animates the dead stone.

The west side of the north cross (Figure 86) has as centre an open flower from which symmetrically arranged small and large spirals emerge and interpenetrate.

Figure 86. The west face of the North Cross of Ahenny.

Figure 87. The west face of the South Cross of Ahenny.
Figure 88. The east face of the South Cross of Ahenny.

The cross as symbol of death is covered by a force field of life that penetrates everything. The cross becomes a 'Tree of Life.' Still today the sweeping lines on the cross at Ahenny can convey some idea of the life-giving effect the crosses once had on men in tune with mythic religion. The same plant-like feeling for life is given by the Ahenny south cross (Figures 87 and 88).

The dragon-animality, the world of the chaotically instinctive, is tamed on the shaft of the cross in a central symmetrical pattern. This animal-dragon being is iniquitous. We find it on the gate of churches (Clonfert), but also surrounding the doorways of Norwegian stave churches (Hedal, Trondheim, Urnes). It lurks in the twisted threads of the initials of the evangelists (Book of Kells), staring with a grimace recorded by the paint brush and pen of a pious monk between the lines of the sacred

Figure 89. Surrounding of a door showing dragon motifs. Norwegian stave church.

text or as a gloss in the margins. They are usually shackled by bonds, tamed and bound.

Germanic mythology knows about the shackling by the gods of light of the Fenris Wolf, the world power of darkness. As long as the 'chains of light' hold the monster, the evil one, he cannot unchain himself in his apocalyptic dimension and bring about the twilight of the gods. Until the nineteenth century the blacksmiths in certain districts in Germany at the end of the day's work used to beat 'three cold blows' on the anvil to harden 'the wolf's chains,' to prevent the animal breaking free.

In the fragment of the cross at Dromiskin (County Louth) even the centre of the 'sun' is overrun and darkened by the plaited tails of the dragon, although they are fettered in the quadrangle.

In the 'Snake-Dragon Cross' at Killamery (County Kilkenny) a dragon dives with gaping jaw from the top against the sun centre of the cross (Figures 90 and 91). It is the adversary of the light, who is attacking the centre of the cross as 'the sun's demon,' as the essence of aggressive darkness. In the two cross-shafts two snakes bite each other with entwined mouths and with their bodies they encircle the clear disc of the sun centre. The centre of light remains untouched. Beneath these dramatic struggles four-leafed flowers grace the rising and 'purified' shaft of the cross. This impressive cross today stands on the lonely ruined site of a monastery which was founded as long ago as the sixth century: Cill Lamhraidhe. The west side clearly displays a sun swastika as the conquering power of the dominating 'centre,' whose spreading rays organize the plaited rays in orderly patterns.

A fourth type of 'interlacing' concerns human beings. There are numerous designs where dragons charge at men or try to swallow them. An early example (Figure 92) is given by the gravestone cross at Gallen Priory (County Offaly). The tails of four dragons are wound round the sun centre with its swastika design. The dragons are attacking the four human heads which are on the ends of the diagonals. The head from time immemorial has been considered the seat of thought and of consciousness. Are the powers of darkness depicted here attacking the minds of men? The human form underneath gives the impression of taking on the threatened struggle. Like a small Atlas he holds up the sun ring with his arms and at the same time his hands touch the dragon's jaws. This stone was the gravestone of a monk. At the same time it points to the inner struggle of the soul as it strives after the Christian ideal.

Figure 90. East face of cross at Kilamery (Kilkenny).
Figure 91. West face of same cross.

Figure 92. The gravestone cross at Gallen Priory (County Offaly).

Figure 93 & 94. Gravestone cross of Carndonagh (County Donegal).

Figure 95. Detail from the first page of Gospel of Luke in the Books of Kells (fol. 188r).

The first page of Luke's Gospel in the 'Book of Kells' shows in detail two 'monks' who incline their heads towards the wide open jaws of two dragons (Figure 95). Clearly this is a voluntary action, and their bearing is that of humility. Braids emerge from the heads of the monks (the realm of thought) which the dragons are biting. Looking at the monk on the left we see how the 'braid of thought' wraps itself round the dragon and how firmly the monk holds the braid in his hand. In the case of the right-hand figure the braid goes from the head (thought) to the mouth (word) and further on to the hand (will). The legs of both are intertwined with each other. Here the human being is living in the world of the dragon, in the world of eclipse. He must insert his thought into it (that is, sacrifice); he does not avoid evil. He has to dare to ponder the thoughts of the Gospel and to meditate amid the threats of the dragon. By the power of thought he can overpower and chain the dragon. The spoken thought, as word (on the right) is able to strengthen the noose which is the manacle. The human being engaged in this task (monk) knows that he is fraternally linked with the other who strives after the same goal (intertwined legs).

The symbolic meaning of the braid motif

The braid is a common theme in all Indo-Germanic cultures. In India the god Varuna was worshipped; he was also known as 'Master of the Bonds.' Varuna placed men who were guilty of being 'tangled' in sins in bonds.[2] Again, it was the

Figure 96. Bronze relief on the Bible of Athlone (County Westmeath).

god Indra's duty to free men 'from bonds': 'That you free those from their bonds, who are bound there.' Tacitus reports this concerning the tribe of the Semnones: 'In another way, too, reverence is paid to the [sacred] grove. No one may enter it unless he is bound with a cord. By this he acknowledges his own inferiority and the power of the deity.'[3] Here the bonds express human inadequacy when facing the world of the divine.

A continuation and elucidation of the braid theme in the Christian period is presented by the text of the old hymn for Good Friday and Easter: 'Christ lay in bonds of death ...' In the rune stone of Jelling (Denmark) the figure of Christ appears on the position of the cross with his entire body fettered by bonds.

The general style of this image suggests an Irish origin. The bonds (braids) are here a symbol for death, for the earthly entanglement and bondage of humanity which Christ has freely chosen to accept. They are the all-embracing bonds of the dragon of darkness and at the same time man in his earth-bound existence. Good Friday's bonds mean the triumph of the forces of death.

Goethe refers to this early Christian symbolism in the Easter Chorus of Faust:

> Christ is arisen
> Out of corruption's womb!
> Burst now your fetters
> Break free from gloom.

Figure 97. The Resurrected One with out-stretched arms. Detail of east face of Moone cross. (See figures 109 and 110).

Figure 98. Christ triumphant over death. East face of South Cross of Durrow (County Offaly).

Figure 99. West face of the South Cross of Durrow.

Figure 100 (opposite). West face of Muiredach Cross at Monasterboice (County Louth).

Figure 101. The West Cross at Kilfenora (County Clare).

Figure 102. The Doorty Cross at Kilfenora.

Figure 103. Simple cross at Monasterboice.

While the braids on the stone in Jelling resemble some Irish crosses and manuscripts in their character of fetters the very ancient cross which is like a gravestone at Cardonagh (County Donegal) displays strong flowing revivifying bands. Here Christ is represented in the aspect of resurrection. Over him is the cross interwoven by every kind of vitalizing coil and plait. Between the coils small round sun symbols are scattered like fruit: the cross at the sun-saturated Tree of Life.

The bronze relief (Figure 96) of the Athlone Bible displays a rare representation of Christ on the cross (seventh century). The large face is a death mask of one who overcomes the suffering and agony of the world. It preserves the moment of 'It is finished' (John 19:30). The spiral of the Trinity rises from the head. The breast, interwoven by the rhythms of beating heart and breath, radiates superphysical life in spiral forms below. Below the centre of the body plaited braids run downwards into the extremities of the limbs and terminate in lively twirling spiral shapes. Above the horizontal cross-shafts of the cross two seraphim portray the link with the world above.

The first stage of holy Irish crosses has the simple shapes of the sun disc and the sun ring. A second stage which is rich in artistry shows orderly streams of light as plaited braids on the sun cross, where the centre of light seems to vitalize and often, soaring in spirals, flows through the braids and tames them to useful order. In later crosses and illuminated manuscripts we encounter the oppressive, bestial

trammelling bands to which even the pious monk sees himself existentially surrendered. In later decorated crosses the figure of Christ himself appears in place of
the symbolic sun centre, for he has overcome all fettering bands.

Main themes on illustrated crosses

Exact dating of Irish stone crosses is seldom possible, because the monks often put
early archaic forms and later ones side by side. A linear, progressive development
cannot be established. Nevertheless the motifs indicate two main periods which
overlapped for centuries.

The first period we have described in the previous chapters. It was a time when
from these works the symbol alone spoke, enriched by the rhythms and the flow of
patterns of the bands and plaits.

In the second period appear pictures of 'illustrations' chiselled in stone. They
always appear in early cultures when symbols lose their force. More imagination is
now demanded of the viewer. The picture relates, interprets opinion, points out the
single, limited event, shows the historical aspect. On the stone crosses appear pictorial accounts of important happenings in both the Old and New Testaments,
which have some connection with the central event on the illustrated cross: the
Good Friday and Easter event. These engraved pictures have a natural resemblance
to a seal. They seem to be like signet rings which try to impress themselves on the
soul of the spectator (see Figures 109–112).

In those days men needed little external pictorial stimulation to make them iden-
tify all their lives with the inner meaning of pictures. These pictures served not only
places of worship but also places for exegesis and for preaching to the community
assembled around the cross. It is known from English sources that the Irish missionaries in Northumbria set up wooden crosses at whose foot they preached the
Gospel.[4]

The figure of Christ on stone crosses

As soon as 'pictures' replace the old symbols no longer do the circular sun symbol,
the sun disc or the swastika stand in the centre of the cross. Now the pictorial transformation of these stands there: the figure of Christ, the incarnation of the forces of
the sun, 'Light of the World.' On Irish stone crosses we never meet with the cruci-
fied figure as a body hanging and subject to gravity which physically 'burdens' the
cross. He is the Risen One, whose radiant expansive appearance hovers, or even the
Giver, the Self-Sacrificer, with lowered arms and bowed head (Figure 97).

In the sun ring of the stone crosses stands Christ, who has overcome death and
continues to exert influence from the spiritual world and helps to lead and endure
the destinies of man 'to the close of the age' (Matt.28:20). So he is represented as

the victor over death, as the Risen One. In his left hand he carries the cross of death, in his right hand the symbol of the Tree of Life, the staff with the two spirals (the Druids' staff), as in Durrow (County Offaly) (south cross, Figure 98), in Kells, in Monasterboice (Figure 52) and Muiredach. In the Book of Kells the Evangelist Luke is portrayed with these signs. On the cross at Kilfenora (County Clare) the Christ figure spreads out his arms in benediction. The sacrificial blood pours down the long shaft of the cross in two streams and spreads over the ground.

An unpretentious cross at Monasterboice (County Louth) shows the radiant Christ sacrificing himself clearly inscribed in a pentagon, a very rare representation (Figure 103). Inside the sun ring the tetrad is in the form of bosses which represent the four Evangelists in conjunction with the Christ. In the Book of Kells (Fol. 290v) and in the images on later crosses (Kells, Figure 107) the four are portrayed. In the Romanesque period their portrayals are numerous.

The transition from crosses with symbols and twisted bands to crosses with picture images lasted centuries and during this period always retained both elements. In some cases one side was still worked in the old symbolic style and the other side with picture images (for instance Castledermot, south cross, Figures 104–106). In other cases surfaces with images interchange with plaited bands, abruptly introducing 'the other vision.' Even where in later times (Monasterboice) pure illustrated crosses are found, the sun-ring is still engraved in the old style with lines and forms of weaving ethereal life.

Examples of illustrated crosses

The Tower Cross of Kells

In the centre of the east side of the Tower Cross (Figure 107) a circular disc with the heptad appears, as on the north cross of Duleek (see p.118). The seven 'bosses' are surrounded by a flowing pattern of rectangular interwoven bands. All four beams have images carved in relief, and only the 'Christ centre' has been left as a numerical symbol. There is an old Irish liturgy in which Christ is called 'Son of the sun, son of the planets ...' The heptad of the centre could represent this, as — including the sun and moon — seven was at that time considered to be the number of the planets.

The sequence of images on the cross cannot be considered accidental if the logical connection of the scenes represented in each case on a side is grasped. It will not be mistaken to take the paradise and Fall scenes as a starting point in each case. This is depicted on almost every cross.

This is also the case here. The Fall appears in the lower part (a scene depicting defection, disloyalty and disobedience) and Cain kills Abel, the beginning of earthly death. Higher up are Shadrach, Meshach and Abednego in the fiery furnace (Dan.3).

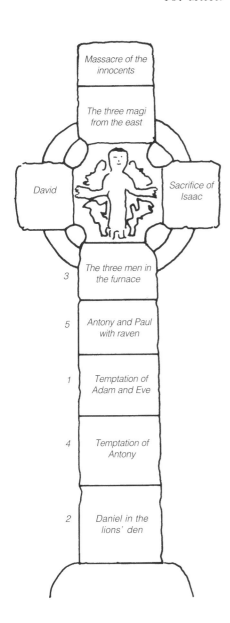

Figure 104. (opposite) The east face of the South Cross of Castledermot (County Kildare)

Figures 105 and 106. The west face of the South Cross of Castledermot

In Babylon they disobeyed the law ordering the worship of the gold image of King Nebuchadnezzar. As punishment they were thrown in a fiery furnace. They survived because divine help was given them by the angel. This is a motif of loyalty standing the test as a direct contrast to the Fall. In the representation of this the same motif is strengthened by one of Daniel in the lions' den. On the left cross-shaft is the sacrifice of Isaac (Gen.22), again the opposite of the Fall. The theme is again obedience and willingness to sacrifice. On the right cross-shaft is the legendary encounter of Paul of Thebes (the hermit) with St Antony.[5] Both are founding Fathers of Egyptian Christianity, and both were highly honoured as hermits even in Ireland. Paul represents the conquest of the flesh by asceticism, Antony the victory over the Tempter's power. At their meeting a raven gave them bread as food from heaven. Although Eve stole the divine food from the tree, she may approach in grace those human beings transformed by Christ. In mythology and legend the raven (Odin's raven) is always a messenger between the earthly and the divine world.

In the top image Christ presides as he breaks bread at the feeding of the five thousand (Matt.14:13–21). Five loaves and two fishes can be seen.

As the centre of the east side indicated in a symbolically veiled way, the west side (Figure 108) portrays Christ in person. On the shaft there is the crucifixion and above this in the centre the Risen One with the emblem of the cross and the Tree of Life, flanked by the tetramorph of the apocalyptic 'beasts,' here portrayed as images which at the same time represent the four Evangelists: angel above (Matthew), bull right (Luke), eagle below (John), lion left (Mark). Above the angel in the medallion is the lamb.

The top image on the cross is a field with twelve bosses; eight small ones, four large ones. This could be a reference to Christ as the 'Lord of the cosmos,' (twelve signs of the zodiac), like the planetary seven on the reverse side in the centre. The four large bosses could correspond to the four cardinal points in the Christian zodiac: angel (Aquarius), Matthew; the bull (Taurus), Luke; the lion (Leo), Mark; eagle (later Scorpion), John. This would show the tetramorph of the evangelists as belonging to the zodiac.

The south cross at Castledermot (County Kildare)

It is assumed that this cross is from the period when the monastery was founded around AD 800. It represents a symbiosis of the entirely geometrical first period and the pictorial second period. The east face (Figure 104) displays interwoven bands and fields of continuous round and angled spirals, which weave through the stone beams with figures of living creatures. The west face (Figure 106) is a pure pictorial cross. Noticeable is the choice of similar images and the way in which with few changes these recur on almost all pictorial crosses. If the intellectual content is examined it becomes clear that they were consciously and deliberately chosen.

Figure 107. The east face of the Cross of Patrick and Columba (Kells, County Meath).

Figure 108. The west face of the Cross of Patrick and Columba, Kells

In the centre of the shaft Adam and Eve succumb to temptation by the Tree of Life (Figure 105, 1). Beneath at the base is Daniel, subduing the lions' loyalty, steadfastness, divine protection (2); associated with this the three men in the fiery furnace (3) as a second Old Testament contrast to the Fall. Immediately below and above Adam and Eve are again (as in Kells) two Christian equivalents: the temptation of Antony (4), and Antony and Paul are receiving divine food from a raven (5). They are men of the new covenant ('Brothers of Christ').

About this developing reunification of the old and new covenants there rises in the aureola of the sun the Easter Christ passing through Good Friday. On his left is Abraham sacrificing Isaac, the original Old Testament image of the highest form of sacrifice. On his right is David playing the harp and singing the hymns of the vast creation and songs from the depths of the human soul. Above the head of Christ are the three kings, and highest of all the innocent children slain at Bethlehem. The religious destinies of the Old and New Testaments are depicted here in a few images. It was the task of the monks to illustrate and emphasize their connection with the Christian mystery by means of such illustrated crosses, for the novices and for the people.

The high cross at Moone (County Kildare)

In the case of each cross the inner logic of the images has to be newly acquired for rational understanding. On the east face (Figures 109 and 110) of this well-preserved cross, which is 5.1 metres (17 feet) high, at eye level on the base is once more the temptation of Adam and Eve. Beneath this is the sacrifice of Isaac as well as Daniel in the lions' den. Above in the sun ring of the cross is the radiant figure of the Risen One, Christ as the 'new Adam.'

Going round the base, on the south face these scenes are found: the three in the fiery furnace, protected by angels; the flight into Egypt (a New Testament theme concerning protection); five loaves, two fishes (symbolic nourishment by Christ).

On the west face (Figure 111) in contrast to the scene of the Fall is the sacrifice of Christ on the Cross, and underneath are the twelve disciples. Above in the ring of this tall cross is the ancient spiral sun swastika, and underneath it is the other pre-Christian symbol of the sun, the lozenge.

In a significant trilogy the north face of the base of the Moone cross (Figure 112) portrays the encounter with the Tempter. Right at the bottom and close to the ground is a fabulous beast with six heads and six feet, shaped like a terrifying double wolf out of which four spiral-shaped dragons grow. It is an image of aggressive darkness and is an example of the pre-Christian mythological representation of evil.

In the panel above it Christ appears in the temptation scene between a dual portrayal of evil. On the left is a goatlike figure of Satan with horns, on the right a

Figures 109 and 110. East face of Moone Cross (County Kildare).

Figure 111. West face of Moone Cross.
Figure 112. Detail of north face of Moone Cross.

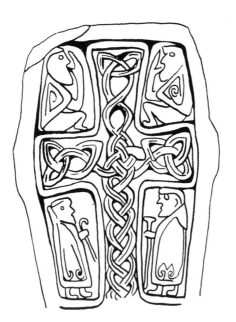

Figure 113. The stele of Drumhallagh (County Donegal).

Figures 114 and 115. The steles of Inishkeel (County Donegal).

birdlike creature with a crest. Christ occupies the centre and is pushing evil to the side.

The panel at the top points to the high cross. It narrows and portrays Paul the hermit with St Antony in the desert. The raven is here a symbol of a changed, subservient animal world. The raven brings the bread (of life) to the hermits and in the centre they are holding this food on their knees.

The main themes of the Moone Cross show, in comparison with those already described, considerable conformity with the canon of images. On other tall crosses we find, in addition to the Old Testament motifs already mentioned, the following: Jacob wrestling with the angels; Jonah and the whale; Moses with the tablets of the commandments; Moses striking water from the rocks; David and Goliath. From the New Testament: the tidings to the shepherds; the worship by the kings; the Baptism in the Jordan; the marriage at Cana; the entry into Jerusalem; the arrest; the crucifixion and resurrection. Only on late crosses, after the spread of Roman Catholic influence, does the Madonna occasionally appear. Old Irish Christianity knew of no real cult of the Virgin Mary.

The stele at Drumhallagh (County Donegal)

On this cross (a tombstone) two basic elements of Old Irish monasticism are present. At the top two men crouch on the left and the right of the braid cross. They are holding their thumbs in their mouths. To such the thumb is the symbol for a person looking into himself, a symbol of meditation. The spirals of their bodies lead to the region of the heart. They are on the way to the 'inner life.' The *vita contemplativa* has found pictorial expression. The aim is to guide the monk through his training into spiritual maturity. It is said of the wise Finn MacCool that he sucked his thumb, and doing this he was able to see hidden things and foretell future happenings.[6]

When the monk had trained and strengthened his soul spiritually by study, tests and meditations, he could rise to a second stage of his life and take up a pilgrim's staff as a missionary. The two lower figures on the tombstone illustrate this. What was depicted at the top as being gained on the path inwards now becomes the force for the outwards path. The flowing spiral has slipped down to the leg of the itinerant missionary, and its determination is carried on the pilgrim's staff into the *peregrinatio*, into the missionary activity.

Conceivably the monk on whose grave this stone was placed had completed his journey on both paths.

The stele at Inishkeel (County Donegal)

One or two symbols present problems. A braided cross tombstone at Inishkeel displays a symmetrical design of riders on swans. This recalls Lohengrin, the

Figure 116. The stele of St Mura of Fahan (County Donegal).
Figure 117. Back of the stele of St Mura, Fahan.

missionary of the Holy Grail. Is it perhaps possible that this almost accidentally surviving symbol indicates that within Irish Christianity in the ninth century there were contacts with the Christian Grail movement?

In any case a 'swan cross' comes from Inishkeel, on which four swans enclose the crosses. (The level of the white swan was regarded as the highest spiritual stage, comparable to that of the white dove.) Parsifal unknowingly killed the swan near the Grail. It is clear to anyone with knowledge of ancient symbols that in this case symbols used are being consciously used and are not mere decorative designs.

The stele of St Mura at Fahan (County Donegal)

On the tombstone of St Mura at Fahan (County Donegal) a Tree of Life rises in intertwined bands, and bears five 'fruits' in the form of sun motifs. At the top is a triangle with a central sun whose rays pour downwards. They are led into the flowing bands of the cross. This illustrates a downward flow of the Logos-light from the region of the heavenly triad (trinity) into the region of the cross, of the earth. Thus the cross of death changes into the Tree of Life, a symbol of the incarnate Logos which animates everything. The stele of St Mura unmistakably illustrates the fact that the intertwined bands in the cross moving down from above are to be understood as bands of light and life.

Summary

A synopsis of the old stone crosses makes it clear that the sun was represented with many variations as descending into the cross. This symbolical and artistic design has four principal forms. In one the sun is a complete disc which is included in the cross of tombstones. In the other type appears the sun symbol which was already used in the megalithic period: the circle with a centre point. It appears on a cross as a sun ring with a central boss. This form can be replaced by a swastika (the sun in movement), it can take the form of a flowering cross, or in its simplest form, as the centre point of a circle. Because the sun is identified with the Logos, with the light of the world, with the Christ, on the cross it has to point out the union of Christ with the earth and with humanity. This is also indicated by the third type of cross where the pictorial cross, the symbol of the centre, is subdivided. Christ appears as a representational form, surrounded by the sun ring or sun disc. (St Valery cross, Fassaroe, County Wicklow). The fourth type of sun cross is constituted by those designs where the forces of the sun flow through the form of the cross in moving lines of light, where the symbol of death is transformed into a Tree of Life. Without exception the Irish sun cross proves to be an Easter Cross, proclaiming the certainty of the unceasing action of the forces of resurrection as the essence of the new Gospel, the spiritual steeping of the earth in the sun as the result of the Christ event.

III

The Spread of Irish Christianity
on the Continent

11. Pelagius, an Early Irish Missionary

From the fifth century onwards there was scarcely any other personality or teaching more disputed in the Christian world than that of Pelagius (c. 370–418). It had supporters and admirers, but still more opponents. The Roman Church condemned him in his own lifetime. 'Pelagianism' became the charge used in the condemnation of every movement towards a churchless Christianity.

In those days the Mediterranean world lumped England, Scotland and Ireland together as Britain. Therefore the nickname 'Brito,' which Augustine gave Pelagius, is no clear indication of his origin. Jerome, however, plainly calls him 'of Irish race, from the region of Britain.'[1]

His original name is not known. According to the custom of the time the peripatetic monks gave themselves a second name. Pelagius is Greek and means 'one who has come over the sea,' and it was appropriate for an Irishman on the Continent. His appearance in Rome (AD 394) was sudden and startling. Apart from his Irish origin as good as nothing is known about his early life and career. He stepped into the light of history as a mature, eloquent and independent individual radiating spiritual power amid Rome's dying and decadent antiquity. At that time the growing Christianity of the South was going through a number of problems of development, and suffering from various personal weaknesses of its representatives. In 333 for reasons of state Emperor Constantine had given religious freedom even to Christians. This had not yet made it possible for the Bishop of Rome in the fourth century to declare that he was 'Pope.' The Eastern Church with Constantinople, Ephesus, and Jerusalem, the 'Africans' with Alexandria, and then of course Rome, all discovered themselves to be differing tendencies in a general movement which was displaying a number of contrary attitudes. Among these were gnosis, Manichaeism and other schools influenced by antiquity, which were introducing into Christianity the most varied theoretical content and cultural forms.

Against Pelagius an opposition was soon to be formed which spread from a central leadership in Rome with the object of bringing the colourful variety of unchristian life into the unified organization of a 'Roman Church.' The appearance of the Christian individualism of Pelagius was the cause of great alarm. In opposition to all ecclesiastical striving for authoritarian power, he represented the Old Irish view and customs. This granted every man the opportunity in religious matters to go his personal, free Christian way.

The 'Petrine' and the 'Johannine' path

After the conversion to Christianity the developing Roman Church at first adopted a policy of reporting miracles and making an impression in this way. By acceptance of miracles and belief in them, belief in the existence of Christ was strengthened. The believer was strengthened still further by being given 'correct doctrine.' This was eventually set out as obligatory in the Creed. Obedience to this could be enforced by the claim to have the authority to define and foster correct doctrines. A Christian in the judgment of this ecclesiastical institution was only one who acknowledged its authority as protector of orthodoxy ('Feed my sheep') and obediently submitted to it. This Petrine path was above all suited to the immaturity of people not yet capable of thoughtful judgment.

There is a great gulf between this attitude and the spirituality of Pelagius. From the nature of Old Irish unecclesiastical Christianity he accepted and propagated an individual path to the Christ mystery. He saw in everyone a spark of spiritual talent that was capable of being developed to an ever greater recognition, contemplation and comprehension of the divine. The education of the ability to think and believe was for Pelagius a means of gradually maturing to spiritual truths. His basic position was trust in man's ability to think. Religious truth and religious error are thinkable and identifiable. This position agrees with the saying of John the Evangelist, who reports Christ's saying: 'You will know the truth and the truth will set you free' (8:32). This is therefore also termed the Johannine position. If this duality is perceived, the influence and fate of Pelagius in the Mediterranean world can be understood.

Appearance in Rome

It must have been about AD 394 when Pelagius arrived on his travels in Rome and as a solitary stranger publicly began his work as a Christian missionary in the city.[2] His tall, athletic and handsome appearance and the power and force of his witty oratory established his reputation. People came in contact with him in the public squares and in the streets, and he had connections with widely differing circles of the city. The Roman lawyer Celestius soon became associated with him. Celestius was at first his pupil and later was at his side for many years as a fellow controversialist and defender, and was also his companion on his journeys. Plinval, an expert on Pelagius, considers Pelagius to have been a reformer in the collapsing Roman Empire, inspiring in his strict observance of the Christian virtues; as a fascinating orator, an original, irrefutable writer, capable of confronting the greatest literary spirits of his century. Outstanding in this category was the Church Father Augustine, the outstanding representative of Petrine Christianity. For though he soon became an outspoken opponent of the works written by Pelagius, he did so as one who recognized Pelagius' spiritual gifts and his course of life.

Pelagius certainly did not pretend to be a representative of any tendency. He struggled completely independently and as an individual for what he considered to be the truth. He made no attempt to recruit supporters or found a school of doctrine. He conversed with such listeners as came to him with an almost Socratic manner about virtue and the Christian life. This method was a novel experience for the Romans. He preached that the consciousness of freedom must be sustained in a man in order that he might find the courage to be virtuous, '... for every noble attempt to achieve fades when we despair of attaining it.'[1]

The theology of Pelagius

His writings

As a result of Pelagius being attacked as a heretic, an attack which began in his lifetime and increased after his death, we have been deprived of most of the originals of his literary work. From quotations and references in ancient sources the following works of Pelagius are known: Three books about the Trinity, *A Book of Witnesses, Discourse in favour of free-will, Letter concerning Grace* (to Bishop Paulin), *Letter to Bishop Constance, Letter to the Consecrated Virgin Demetria, Commentary on the Letters of Paul.*[4]

After his death an anti-Pelagian revision of some of his works was grotesquely undertaken. These carry the name Primarius. These fraudulent versions were used to combat this unwelcome, disturbing figure from the north more effectively, a spirit which had dared to live a free apostleship based on its own resources.

Some of his text has survived, for in order to refute him, Augustine quoted him frequently and at length. It is a fact, however, that 'scholarship has all too often taken its judgment of the heresiarch Pelagius from the polemic of Augustine and consequently has accepted a distorted view.'[5] G. F. Wiggers rendered a great service by publishing a thorough treatment of the controversy between Augustine and Pelagius.

The meaning of Christ

In his dispute with Arianism Pelagius asserts that they misunderstood the 'true divinity' of Christ.[6] Opposing the Manichees he asserts that they misunderstand the 'true human nature' of Christ. For Pelagius, Christ is the incarnate Logos, in the Johannine sense. Father and Son are *una operatio* (of one creation). Again, Pelagius speaks of Christ as the unwearying, resurrected Logos in the same sense as Paul. Christ is for him both a spiritual and a historical being. He compares the Old

Testament with the light of the moon, which inspired Moses and Elijah, as a reflection of the Logos of the Sun. The New Testament was for him the messenger of the sun, of the Christ. He recognized that here again is the symbolic and figurative representation of Christ found in the Irish stone crosses.

The nature of Man

Pelagius does not view the vital question of good and evil in Man (light and darkness) brought into Christianity by Manichaeism as determinist and immutable as does Augustine. The Fall and the descent into matter form, according to Pelagius, an evolutionary path on which the spiritual leadership of mankind takes part.[7] The situation of mankind gradually changed 'after Adam's Fall,' as sins became more widespread and human nature became darker. Accordingly for Pelagius the human body was not an evil in itself. On the contrary he spoke of a *sensus carnalis*, sensual emotion which can lead away from the divine and which is able to ensnare Man in many ways. But 'creative grace' is now given to mankind, and man can as a result carry out an inner change and liberation from evil in himself with the strength of his spirit. The possibility of using this freedom is for Pelagius a 'gift of the Logos,' of the Christ. 'Freedom of will is the ornament of the rational soul.'[8]

The man who 'despises grace'

One of the main arguments used in the polemical accusations of heresy which were made against Pelagius was that he was guilty of being one who 'despised grace' and praised an arrogant self-redemption achieved by freedom of will. How unjust this was to Pelagius can be shown by his teachings on grace.[9] Pelagius distinguished three types of grace, which were for him acquired perceptions.

Creative grace was grace of the Logos: The ability to do good deeds deriving from the spirit embedded in human beings, the capacity for free will, the gift of speech.

Revelation's grace in pre-Christian thought was the grace of the Law which made it possible to know the divine will, before human beings could recognize it and find it from their own resources. In post-Christian thought it is the 'Grace of Christ's revelation' *sine lege* (without law) to which free efforts can lead.

Grace of forgiveness, grace of baptism: by entering the brotherhood of Christ through baptism human beings can experience a sense of being changed each day and they experience the growth of perception in themselves. This makes it possible for them to build a new person of themselves that can recover from the influence of evil deeds and grow out of them.

Pelagius did not set the human being in a subjective struggle for salvation. For him humans were rather a single limb of a general development of a Christianized humanity, in which each individual is called upon to co-operate and work. Humanity can become the body of Christ, although Pelagius says: 'We are not the body of Christ if we behold the separation of one of its limbs without suffering.'[10]

Augustine against Pelagius

If in Pelagius' views a high value of the human being and his religious strivings is found, it is rooted in recognition of the threefold spiritual gifts of the human individual, the opposite of which can be found in Augustine. In AD 400 his *Confessions* appeared which revealed the subjective struggle of his soul, which had matured amid pagan and Manichaean concepts, with the Christian revelation. The individual has no meaning here. He merely plays a part in a great universal court of judgment which goes beyond him and where he has humbly to accept what has been decided about him. Augustine accordingly complains that Pelagius does not admit that unbaptized children are damned. After Adam's Fall everyone, for Augustine, is in a state of original sin and therefore completely doomed. 'Every man therefore brings into the world a nature already in so ruined a condition that he is not only more inclined to evil than to good but he is not capable of anything else but sin.'[11] Augustine's doctrine of the soul concentrates as though spellbound on the sinful part of man, the negative part of the soul. Pelagius looks at the positive side of man, on the ability to surmount sin, 'There is in our hearts, if I may so express it, a certain natural holiness which both keeps watch in a fortress of the soul and judges good and evil..'[12]

And in the letter to Demetria:

> In the freedom to choose between good and evil exists the distinction of the rational soul; in this is the honour of our nature, its dignity and worth ... We deny the Lord, if we say, it is difficult, we cannot, we are human beings ... O blind madness! O unholy audacity! ...
>
> The potential of (human) nature God always supports with help from his grace .... Then he opens the eyes of our hearts. Reason is impressed on our soul as the image of the Creator, to his dignity freedom of the will also belongs ... with free will does Grace effect its help.[13]

It is astonishing how Pelagius with his Irish background understands and handles the vocabulary and concepts of southern theology, which he combines with his positive, liberating Christianity and encourages the bold and confident striving of Man. Nevertheless, there was great opposition. More and more clearly Augustine opposed Pelagius, as weak and simple. He wants to be the guardian of a strict 'pure doctrine' and at the same time he identifies himself with the work of a vicarious orthodox Church.

The encounter between the two contestants

In the year 411 Pelagius and his faithful companion Celestius travelled by way of Sicily and the Mediterranean to North Africa, despite Augustine's attacks. It is proof of his inner greatness that he dared to make an attempt at an understanding and risk a dangerous journey across the sea, although the chance of success was small, as Augustine's influence was so great.

In Carthage a meeting took place between Augustine and Pelagius. Unfortunately no account of this important moment in the history of the world has come down to us. The sole information we have is that shortly afterwards Pelagius continued on his journey to Jerusalem, while his companion Celestius remained in Carthage. No resolution of their differences was possible. Before his departure Pelagius wrote a letter to Augustine which has been lost but which received a courteous answer. In it he calls Pelagius 'Dominum dilectissimum et desideratissimum fratrem,' (the highly esteemed gentleman and much sought-after brother).[14]

This expression of his esteem did not prevent Augustine from getting this troublesome individual expelled from the Church at a synod in Carthage in 412, and the Pelagian doctrine condemned as heresy. Celestius attempted to go on working in Carthage as a free apostle for some while after the departure of Pelagius.

Pelagius in Jerusalem

With the important stages of his life of trouble — Ireland, Rome, Alexandria, Carthage and Jerusalem — Pelagius had completed a significant diagonal stretching from the north west (Ireland) across Europe through Rome to the Near East. This must have inspired in him the idea of a brotherhood of all Christians. Coming from a Christendom which up till then had been the goal of spiritual striving, he now found himself in Jerusalem treading the ground of its historical origin. The Patriarch John of Jerusalem belonged to the Eastern Church. It was a question of decisive importance whether Pelagius could come to agreement with him. Astonishingly this did occur. The encounter occurred with a good omen. In the shortest possible time a friendship developed between these two important representatives of early Christian movements. Patriarch John defied Augustine's condemnation and defended the missionary who had travelled so far from home. It must have been one of the most sublime experiences for Pelagius to find inner understanding and spiritual friendship here on the site which held memories of the historical Christ.

Not far from Jerusalem, St Jerome had a monastery. He had spent some years in Rome and was considered a fanatical ascetic. Jerome sided against Pelagius and in favour of Augustine. Pelagius had not founded a school in Jerusalem and made no attempt to make converts there. He lived there according to his Christian convictions, simply but intensely. He called himself the worst of sinners. Nevertheless

Jerome attacked him very crudely. In the preface to his commentary of Jeremiah (first book) this passage concerning Pelagius can be read: '...that ignorant traducer who ... thought it worth his while to censure my commentaries on Paul's Epistle to the Ephesians. The stupid fool, labouring under his load of Scotch porridge, does not recollect what we said ....'[15]

In the preface to the third part of this commentary he writes: '... he barks like a mountain dog of immense bodily size (*per alpinum canem, grandem et corpulentum*) who can tear better with his claws than with his teeth. He is of Irish race, from the region of Britain ....'[16]

The dramatic year of 415 came. In Alexandria a Christian mob was incited to attack Hypatia, the brilliant heathen teacher of ancient wisdom, and trampled her to death. In the same year Augustine sent his young, fanatical representative Orosius to Jerusalem to oppose Pelagius and to bring about his downfall also at a synod of the Eastern Church. Augustine's great opponent was to be accused also in Jerusalem of heresy. The Council met at the end of July. The Patriarch John presided, Orosius appeared as the prosecutor. The youthful fanatic uttered his charges and sarcastic comments in Latin which had to be translated, as Greek was the language of the Council. Amongst other matters, he quoted Job 15:25–27: 'Because he has stretched forth his hand against God, and bids defiance to the Almighty, running stubbornly against him with a thick-bossed shield; because he has covered his face with his fat, and gathered fat upon his loins.' Pelagius replied in fluent Greek and convincing argument. He and his defenders remained silent about certain charges, and consequently Jerome tried to make fun of the 'dumb dogs who wanted to bark but no longer knew how.'[17]

In spite of this type of mockery the spiritual issues were clear and the Synod of Jerusalem declared that Pelagius was not guilty of heresy. Nevertheless it was decided that if the matter became an important cause of dispute with Roman Catholicism, then it should be referred to Rome.

St Jerome made the angry comment that it would have been sufficient for Pelagius to stamp his foot, frown with flashing eyes, gesticulate and pour out a torrent of words for darkness to spread immediately before the eyes of the judges.[18]

In December of the same year there was another Synod of the Eastern Church, for Pelagius was given no peace. The Synod was summoned to Diospolis (ancient Lydda, north-west of Jerusalem) by Eulogius, the Primate of Palestine. The Patriarch John of Jerusalem was among the fourteen Palestinian bishops.[19] At Orosius' side two 'Gallic bishops' appeared in Jerusalem, and they also took part in the Synod of Diospolis. They brought a new and stronger indictment. Pelagius refuted most of this as misrepresentation, wrong construction and false interpretation of his writings. A complete record of this synod exists, on which Plinval makes the comment:

Against the strength of his conviction his opponents could not prevail, nor could the condemnations by authorities. His frankness often offended, but his vigour and the clarity of his ideas vindicated him. His logic was convincing, his eloquence delightful. Strong and powerful forces radiated from him, which others could not ignore.'[20]

Pelagius was acquitted at this synod of the charges (self-redemption, contempt for grace, ignoring original sin, and so on) and as a result he was understood and protected by the Eastern Church in the second great controversy. In the record of the Synod of Diospolis are the following passages from Pelagius's defence: '... I assert that a man who has been converted from sin could by his own efforts and the grace of God be without sin ... God gives a power of grace to those who are worthy. Others can be blessed as Paul was.'[21]

For Augustine, whose envoys had been unsuccessful against Pelagius in the synod, the acquittal was a defeat. In a sermon dealing with this question he raged: 'The heresy has not been acquitted, only the man who denied the heresy.' As a result of this shock, in 416 he summoned to Carthage a Synod with sixty-eight bishops, most of whom were not members of the Eastern Church. He achieved what he wanted: the unconditional condemnation of Pelagius and the confirmation of the original condemnation at Carthage in 412.

Rome as the final court of appeal

Since the Eastern Church had clearly broken with Augustine by acquitting Pelagius, Augustine wrote to the Bishop of Rome, Innocent I (402–417), after the verdict of condemnation by the Synod of Carthage and requested him to give his view of the case.[22] Innocent was delighted to be appealed to as arbitrator and exploited this opportunity to declare the See of Rome the highest Court of Appeal in questions of doctrine, and condemned Pelagius, Celestius and the doctrine of Pelagius on the grounds which Augustine had suggested to him. Until then the Bishop of Rome was not yet universally acknowledged as Pope and head of the Catholic Church. The 'Africans' in particular with their centres of Alexandria and Carthage emphasized their own sovereignty. Innocent evaluated the situation which had now developed. He wrote, '... that nothing in the whole world was to be decided without the cognizance of the See of Rome; in particular in questions of doctrine all bishops would have to turn to St Peter' (that is, the Bishop of Rome, the Pope).[23]

The decision of the See of Rome in favour of the Augustinian position evoked the great joy and satisfaction of the African bishops. They even suppressed their desire for independence. Augustine proclaimed from the pulpit that Pelagius had now been condemned by two Councils and the Apostolic See (*Sermons* 131, c.10). Quite astonishingly in the struggle against Pelagius the authority of Rome had been consolidated at a stroke.

Innocent died two months later. His successor, Zosimus (417–418), proved to be not impartial. Celestius, Pelagius' comrade in arms, hurried from Constantinople to Rome and appealed to Zosimus against the condemnation of Pelagius. Pelagius himself wrote from Jerusalem to Rome and enclosed a statement of his doctrine. Zosimus organized a fresh Synod in Rome which rehabilitated Pelagius. For a short time a situation developed in which Pelagius brought Ireland, Rome, Jerusalem, apart from the Augustinian 'Africans,' into harmony. The divergence of trends was suddenly linked with an 'axis' of Christian agreement which ran across Europe as far as Jerusalem.

Zosimus informed the 'Africans' of the vindication of Pelagius in a letter. This communication had a sensational effect and sent waves of indignation through the ranks of the bishops who supported Augustine. In November 417 they convened a huge synod attended by 217 bishops and here the condemnation of Pelagius was renewed. As a result pressure was brought to bear on Zosimus. In Rome the monk Constantinus staged a 'rising of the people' against Zosimus' friendly attitude towards Pelagius, which probably became violent. The opponents of Pelagius had at the same time gained the support of Honorius, the Emperor living at Ravenna. For his part he threatened Zosimus that he would march on Rome with his army if he refused to condemn Pelagius. Zosimus surrendered to force and in April 418 had to accept the issue of the 'Ravenna Decree' against those who 'disturbed the peace of the Church.' In it was decreed 'by an irrevocable law' that the leaders of this infamous doctrine, Celestius and Pelagius, must immediately be banished from the city and 'those people, too, who showed they are supporters of this blasphemy ... let them be where they will, be they laymen or priests, they are to be seized and accused by everyone and mercilessly punished with exile.'[24] In a later supplement the confiscation of the possessions of 'Pelagians' was decreed as the punishment.

We do not know how the banishment of Pelagius from the city of Rome was carried out, nor where he went. Nothing more was heard of him. This year of 418 was considered to be the year of his death. Nothing is known of his grave. He arrived like a comet and unflinchingly strove for a Johannine Christianity. In like manner he vanished again into the unknown.

Another Synod in Carthage in 418 pronounced an even sharper anathema, and from then on Pelagianism was equated with arch-heresy. Under the pressure of these events Zosimus completed his change of attitude by recognizing the doctrine of Augustine as the correct creed. In 418 he issued the *Epistola Tractoria*, in which the errors of Pelagius were set out and their condemnation pronounced. Still in the same year Zosimus was succeeded by Boniface I.

Every bishop in Italy had to sign the *Epistola* against Pelagius. There were, however, seventeen bishops who refused to sign, chief among them Julian, Bishop of Eclanum, in Apulia. These seventeen supporters of Pelagius were deposed by imperial command

and exiled from Italy. In vain they complained that 'they had not been allowed to defend themselves before learned judges but had been ill-treated by the rowdy and ignorant mob, and that their opponents had used the secular arm against them where the help of reason would be denied them.'[25] The methods of those who persecute opinions and beliefs do not change for thousands of years.

On June 9, 419 a joint decree was issued by the Emperors Honorius of the West and Theodosius II of Byzantium, in which those people were to be included in the persecution 'who failed to drive out or denounce secret Pelagians.' From now on every troublesome citizen or anyone who thought in any way independently could be accused of Pelagianism and persecuted, and in the following century this happened often enough. The internal Christian persecution from now on used methods of power and as a result the orthodox Church came to rely more and more on intolerant and exclusive authority. The early Christian attitude disappeared. This had been expressed by St Ambrose of Milan (c. 339–397) in the word: 'The heart of such a great mystery can never be reached by one sole path.'

A few years after the death of Pelagius, Prosper of Aquitaine reported:

> Pope Celestine (422–432) was very severe against the promoter of Pelagianism. He delivered the British lands from the disease with much zeal; there were enemies of grace living in those places where it had its origin; he even drove them out of the most distant areas into the ocean.[26]

A Gallic synod (c. 428) decided to send the bishops Germanus (c. 378–448) and Lupus of Troyes (c. 383–479) to Britain to combat Pelagianism. The delegation travelled there in 429 and in particular visited the district of Hadrian's Wall in the north. This first wave of persecution showed that southern Christianity wanted to have nothing in common with northern Christianity and that it was incapable of tolerating it.

This victory of the Roman Papacy shattered one of the many attempts to bring into the development of the young Church a belief in the individual's freedom of conscience. In this dispute Augustine had played the decisive role:

> He opposed anything that suggested in any way that connection with a spiritual world or with the Christ could come out of the individual human initiative. His efforts were directed to developing the Church gradually into an external institution .... The individual human being had no part of it but an accumulation of abstract dogmas and concepts was imposed on the individual human being.[27]

In contrast to this the spiritual emphasis of Irish Christianity was on the principle of individuality and the 'Church' as an institution was not regarded as important. The growing power of the Roman Church had to reject this view, and in the case of Pelagius, to condemn it.

The fate of Pelagius has concerned men for centuries. It recalls Goethe's statement which reflects his own attitude to the Church:

> That which separated me from the [Moravian] Brotherhood, as well as from other worthy Christian souls, was just that on which the Church has already more than once fallen into dissension. One part maintained by the fall of man human nature has been so far corrupted that to its innermost core not the least trace of good was to be found in it, therefore, man must renounce his own powers altogether and expect everything from grace and its influence. The other part very willingly admitted the hereditary defects of mankind, but wished to attribute to nature a certain inward germ which, animated by divine favour, was able to grow up to a joyous tree of spiritual happiness. With this conviction I was penetrated to my inmost soul without knowing it myself ...
>
> This very thing they maintained against me was genuine Pelagianism, and to the misfortune of modern times this corrupting doctrine was again prevailing. At this I was astonished and alarmed. I went back to Church history, reflected more closely on the doctrine and fate of Pelagius, and now saw clearly how these two irreconceivable opinions had fluctuated hither and thither ...[28]

12. Patrick in the Twilight of History and Legend

No figure in Old Irish Christianity has been so obscured by legend as that of St Patrick, who today is still presented in encyclopedias and historical works as the first and sole founder of Irish Christianity. Legends can illuminate and shed light on historical figures — Francis of Assisi, for example — when they stem from the powerful vibrations of a remarkable personality. By means of images and allegories their deeper essence is then brought closer to the hearts of plain men, of the people. But legends can also obscure a historical figure when they come from a tendentious desire to create significance for a personality in order to use it for a definite purpose.

Patrick is an example of this. Forgotten for a very long time he was brought into prominence two hundred years after his death as the 'first founder' of Old Irish Christianity, and even of its 'Roman character.' And according to some accounts this Christianity derives solely from Patrick and after him, it is alleged, it spread over Ireland. This thesis, which the Roman Catholic Church has adhered to for a century, can no longer be historically sustained. Nevertheless, Patrick remains an important Irish missionary of the fifth century, although Irish Christianity already existed before Patrick.

Armagh was founded as a Roman Catholic centre in the eighth century when the Roman Church wanted to free Ireland from heathen and Pelagian remnants of errors and to get rid of the old traditional Christianity. Patrick was chosen as the director of this work of reform. And so in the eighth century there arose in the course of a few decades dozens of legends which portrayed Patrick as the missionary from the southern, Roman world.[1] In some of these he was even said to have come from Rome with the Pope's blessing. In this way he was promoted to the position of symbol and central figure of Roman-Irish Christianity, which from the eighth century on gradually Romanized all Ireland.

It is highly probable that when Patrick was in Gaul he tried to make contact with the most important Christian centre in Gaul, the Island of Lérins which lies off Cannes. Honoratius, a Burgundian noble, had absorbed Greek Christian spirituality when travelling in Greece. In AD 375 he and his companions founded a centre on the island to which even monks from the Near East thronged. After the dispute with Pelagius had taken place, Lérins became in Rome's view the centre of the heresy of Semi-Pelagianism. For some time Hilary of Arles and Germanus of Auxerre worked here as well. According to tradition Patrick had stayed with the last named. Another important figure was the Breton Faustus who became Abbot of Lérins in 433 and

Figure 118. St Patrick and a King, miniature from a manuscript (vellum). Huntington Library and Art Gallery, California, USA.

was later Bishop of Riez. He too was a contemporary of Patrick, and they may have met. Faustus wrote in a letter about monastic life: 'What we are seeking here is not rest, is not security; it is dispute and struggle ... that finds its scene and action in us. That is the cause which has led us to this peaceful isolation: spiritual battle.'[2] Lérins was, in fact, consciously non-Augustinian. The aim here, as in Ireland, was to bring human freedom into harmony with Christianity and there was accordingly a commitment to the Johannine tendency.

Caesarius, a distinguished abbot of Lérins, was ordained bishop by the Pope in Rome in 512 and was won over to the Augustinian viewpoint, and with him independent Gallic Christianity came to an end. In the seventh century the Rule of St Benedict was introduced and overcame the last resistance. The Christian school of Lérins which inspired Patrick, and which had been independent of Rome, was at last integrated.

It is only possible, therefore, to form a true idea of Patrick if it is supported by the two sources generally recognized today as authentic. These are his *Confession* and a surviving *Epistle to Coroticus*, a chieftain in Northumbria.[3] The authenticity of these sources should still less be doubted because in some important respects their content differs from the contentious view of Patrick which was later devised. These sources had therefore for the most part been overlooked, hushed up, and at times misinterpreted. They were therefore certainly not written to express the Church's view of Patrick. Before the outline of Patrick's life which comes from these sources is described the astonishing fact must be recorded that there is no historical evidence of his grave, and that no school, monastery or particular tradition is certain to have derived from him which continued significantly after his death. There is no evidence of any churches founded by him, or of any places where he founded churches. Historians have conjectured that the northern part of Ireland was his sphere of activity.

Even for the main centre of Armagh attributed to him there is no historical evidence that can be dated before his death. It was appointed a centre of Patrick more than two hundred years later, as part of an effort to assign a place of work to the revered Irish apostle which at the same time could be developed into a prominent centre for subsequent Romanization.

The *Confession* of Patrick has the following outline of his life: Patrick's father, Calpurnius, was an official in the Roman administration of Britain in 400. He was a Christian and like his grandfather before him looked after a Christian community. His Celtic name is said to have been Sukket, Sukkat or Sochet. Patrick accounts for his own somewhat imperfect Latin as a result of laziness as a child. As the son of a Roman official he must have had some schooling. Patrick also produces the excuse that he had again forgotten his Latin during his later imprisonment in Ireland.

In the year 405 the Irish King Niall ventured upon a warlike expedition to Britain.

Among many prisoners he also brought the sixteen-year-old Patrick to slavery in Ireland. He was sold to a man named Miliuc in the County of Antrim. For six years he looked after this man's herds. He lived among Christians there. This shows that there was Christianity in Ireland before Patrick came. Patrick gives no more information about this.

His religious feeling had been deepened by contemplative meditation and this led to visionary experiences. In his *Confessions* we read:

> But after I came to Ireland — and so tended sheep every day, and often prayed in the daytime ... up to a hundred prayers and at night nearly as many, and I stayed in the forest, and on the mountain, and before daylight I used to be roused to prayer in snow and frost and rain, and felt no harm, nor was any inclination to take things easily in me, because, as I see now, the spirit seethed in me.[4]

He twice experienced a call to escape. Accordingly he wandered away to the distant sea coast. There he found the ship which had appeared to him in a vision and on which he was to leave Ireland. Some days later he landed or beached the ship on an uninhabited coast (Brittany?). Patrick and his shipmates roamed and starved for many days through a land devoid of people. They wandered about for twenty-eight days before encountering anyone and obtaining food.

> Well, on that same night I was sleeping and Satan tempted me powerfully, which will be a memory as long as I am in this body, and he fell on me like a great rock (while) nothing in my limbs had any strength. But how did it occur to me in my ignorance to call upon Helias? And meanwhile I saw the sun rise in the sky, and while I shouted Helia! Helia! with all my might, lo and behold the splendour of that sun fell down on me and at once smashed off all the weight from me; and I believe I was helped by Christ my Lord ...[5]

After this Patrick left his companions. He speaks of a second period of captivity. It is not known where he travelled on his wandering in Gaul. He may have been in touch with Gallic Christians. The pseudo-sources, the so-called *Dicta Patrici*, which tell of a journey through Gaul and Italy to the islands of the Tyrrhenian Sea, are not trustworthy. Lérins and Auxerre are also mentioned. The *Confessions* has no evidence at all to support this.

It is certain, though, that he only returned to Britain many years later. There his Irish friend Victoricus appeared to him in a vision, a man he had known in the days of his captivity there. In this vision Victoricus gave him a letter whose opening words were 'The Voice of the Irish.' As he read the letter Patrick heard the voices of the inhabitants of the Wood of Foclut. These voices cried: 'We beg you, holy boy, to come and walk among us once again.'[6] This experience decided Patrick to return to Ireland against the wishes of his followers. It is not known what other factors influenced his decision, although there are many hypotheses. Patrick must have reached Ireland again in about 432. In his *Confessions* he says that his motive was that a sin of his youth had to be expiated by missionary work in Ireland. There is no evidence that he really was concerned with ecclesiastical initiation. He speaks himself of religion as an inner experience. 'And another time I saw him praying inside me as it seemed ... So I believe! — because of his indwelling spirit, which has worked through me ever since that day.'[7]

It is not disputed that he was acquainted with Gallo-Roman Christianity. In the *Confessions* he also relates that he met Christians after his return to Ireland and that he also came across Christians in remote regions 'where no one had yet come to baptize.' Patrick therefore must have carried out ceremonies of baptism. Delius considers it possible that in Gaul Patrick had been ordained as a presbyter.[8]

In the second important source, the *Epistle to Coroticus*, a chieftain in Northumbria, who overran an Irish Christian settlement and was admonished by Patrick, he makes one of the most important statements concerning the state of pre-Patrick Christianity. Patrick wrote: 'In the days of old, the law of God was already well planted and propagated in Ireland; I do not wish to take credit for the work of my predecessors; I share the task of all those whom God has called and foreordained to preach the Gospel ...'[9] In another passage in this letter he points out that the Christians he met in Ireland 'had come to Christianity of their own accord.'

Patrick's statement in the middle of the fifth century that 'Christianity in Ireland was already implanted in ancient times' could agree with the theory of an inspired experience by special personalities that began in the first century. The second statement is nearer to the hypothesis that Patrick was referring to actual experience of visions, such as he mentioned in the *Confessions* as his own experience.

If one also considers the passage where Patrick says, 'I did not wish to take credit for the work of my predecessors,' it appears that Patrick had definite knowledge of his predecessors and their influence in the first centuries and knew that he was only the man newly appointed to continue the work of Christianizing which had begun long ago.

In the *Vita* of Declan five bishops officiating before Patrick are listed: Ibar, Abban, Declan, Aible and Cieran the Elder. The *Vita* says of St Abban:[10]

His relations and friends were astonished at the high quality of his life and habits and would say to each other: 'What kind of boy can this be? He has not been taught by any man, and yet is able to carry out the works done by monks with long experience, and he can also instruct the learned?' Contrary to the wishes of his father, an Irish king, he was brought up to serve Christ. [11]

If one considers evidence of this kind alongside the appearance of Pelagius as a learned emissary, whose Greek and Latin were of such a high order that he was able to defend his free, Northern Christianity eloquently and to express it in written treatises, then it must be realized that we are looking at phenomena of Irish culture that belonged to the Old Christianity that preceded Patrick. This culture and its documents were almost completely washed away by numerous wars with invaders. Pelagius and Patrick are important if very different witnesses to the Christian culture of the earliest centuries in Ireland.

13. Irish Missionaries

As has been explained, it was characteristic of Old Irish Christianity to place particular stress on the two monkish virtues: the practice of the inner life of meditation as well as daily activity and preaching in the world outside. The *vita contemplativa* was the pre-condition for the later entry into the Whitsuntide *vita activa*, obeying the missionary charge: 'go into all the world ...' (Mark 16:15).

Twenty-five missionaries left Ireland for Scotland, 44 for England, 81 for Gaul, 115 for the Germanies and 13 for Italy.[1] Jonas, Columbanus' biographer, mentions that more than 600 missionaries set out from Luxeuil alone (the monastery founded by Columbanus in the Vosges). These numbers may indeed be incomplete and inexact, but they do give some indication of the manifold vitality the Irish monks brought to the conversion of the west.

Many examples are known of monks withdrawing and becoming anchorites in the second half of their lives, above all on the West Coast of Ireland and on small outlying islands. Their object was to deepen their Christian way of life by asceticism and mysticism. An alternative decision was an oath voluntarily to leave their beloved Irish homeland and become a homeless wanderer on the Continent to convert the heathen and to spread the Gospel of Christ. This freely chosen pilgrimage of teaching was considered to be a higher and more exacting level of Christian life which was undertaken as a test.

At times it happened that an Abbot imposed peregrination on a monk as a punishment.[2] It came about therefore that there were also lonely erring pilgrims atoning for their sins who went to the heathen and did not know where to lay their heads. They wandered in twos, in threes, in groups of seven or even in bands of twelve and following the example of Christ with the thirteenth member as leader. This has become known from Columbanus and Willibrord. The pilgrimage of preaching seldom had a definite missionary goal. The monks surrendered themselves completely to uncertainty and would found a monastery anywhere. From the sixth to the ninth century the Irish or Scots monasteries had flourished all over Northern Europe. (*Scotus* at that time was used as much as a name for Irish as for Scots.)

Dicuil, an Irish scholar at the court of Charlemagne writes in his *De Mensura Orbis Terrae* about AD 800 that the Faroe Isles had been inhabited by Irish settlers for hundreds of years. Icelandic tradition knows that Iceland was converted to Christianity before the coming of the Vikings.[3] On Iceland old Irish parchments, bells and bishops' staffs have been found.

The number of Irish monastic foundations is so great that only a few instances can be cited here to indicate their character. Details can be found in Delius or more comprehensively in Ebrard.[4]

The whole available range of modern research leads to the conclusion that the establishment and growth of Christianity took place in Ireland during the first centuries after Christ and developed such strength that it drove on to expand in Northern Europe in the following centuries.

Ninian: the first contact with Rome

The first traces of Roman Christianity came to Britain with the Roman legions in the third and fourth centuries. The son of a baptized tribal chief in the district around the Solway Firth is said to have stayed in Rome and on his journey home to have stayed with Martin of Tours.[4] In 397 he built the monastery Candida Casa at Whithorn, in his own country, on the model of Martin's monastery at Tours. It became the missionary centre in an extensive heathen region north of Hadrian's Wall. It is possible that this resulted in the first appearance of antagonism between the Irish Christianity which had penetrated Britain and the Romanizing Ninian. Delius remarks: 'Ninian's task, however was not to convert his homeland to Christianity but to combat heresy in Britain ... Probably Pelagianism, too, had entered the island.'[5]

By Pelagianism, however, Rome meant in particular that free Christianity, of which Pelagius, Ninian's contemporary, had been a representative. A later reconciliation by Ninian with this Irish independence is perhaps indicated by his favourable inclusion as a 'church founder' in the Irish martyrology, *Félire Óengus.*[6]

The fall of the Roman Empire and the accompanying migrations destroyed contact with Candida Casa and the missionary work which Ninian had begun. The after-effects died away, and as a result Columcille had to convert Scotland and Northumberland afresh from Iona in the sixth century.

Columba (Columcille)

A central figure in the sixth century Old Irish Christianity, the founder of important monastic communities and churches, is Crimthann mac Felim, who was born in Donegal about 521 in a royal family (Ceneiconaill). He later adopted the name of Columba. The King of Tara was his uncle. The Irish honoured this Columba as Columcille, Dove of the Church. An early and reliable biographer, Adamnan, was himself able to hear the opinions of his pupils and gives this description of him.

> Angelic in appearance, elegant in address, holy in work, with talents of the highest order and consummate prudence, ... He never could spend the space of even one hour, without study, or prayer, or writing, or some other holy occupation, and so incessantly was he engaged night and day, in the unwearied exercise of watching and of corporal austerities, that the weight of his

singular labour would seem beyond the power of all human endurance. And still he was beloved by them all, for a holy joy ever beaming on his face, revealed the ecstasies with which the Holy Spirit filled his inmost soul.[7]

Adamnan gives various accounts of the spirituality of his appearance. He said to one man who marvelled at it: 'Heaven has granted some people the grace of seeing plainly and clearly in their spirit the whole earth, the wide sea and all the sky.'

He had a monastic education at Molville and later at Clonard. There is historical evidence that in 563 he left Ireland with some companions in boats and chose Iona, an island off the coast of Scotland, as the site for his further activities. This place soon emerged as a centre as a result of spiritual enterprise and energy. The original name of the island was Hy. Iona, which is the Hebrew word for a dove, may have been the name given to the island by the monks.

From here Columba and his companions made missionary journeys in Scotland. He converted Brude, the king of the northern Picts. The King of the Scots, Aidan, was ordained by him the priest on Iona. Columba later went with him to Ireland with the object of establishing friendly relations with the high king there. Among the many monasteries founded in Ireland by Columba the two important monasteries of Durrow (County Offaly) and Derry are mentioned.

In the Irish assembly at Drumceat (*c.* 575) he moved that the Scottish king, who was still under Irish suzerainty, should become independent of the motherland (Ireland) forever. In this way Columba shared in the foundation of an independent kingdom of Scotland. From his base on Iona Columcille actively influenced Scotland as a teacher and missionary for thirty-four years, and he was responsible for more and more tribes adopting Christianity.

It was at this assembly, too, that Columcille defended the old original organization of bards, which had been infiltrated by various parasitical groups. He helped to return their former prestige to the bards by stricter selection and the foundation of new bardic schools.

In Columcille the qualities of priest, scholar, poet and statesman were united. In his time, therefore, he had the moral authority of a spiritual leader over the 'invisible Irish Church.' Ludwig Bieler observes: 'Down to the eighth century Columba and his successors held a place of honour within the Irish Church that was challenged by none.'[8]

Columcille died on June 9, 597, after his namesake Columbanus and twelve companions had settled on the Continent at a centre at Luxeuil. According to legend Columbanus has spent some time on Iona as a pupil of Columcille and had been given the task of going to the mainland as a missionary. This cannot be proved by historical evidence, but this does not mean that there was no meeting between the two.

Several missionaries are known to have travelled from Iona and founded monastic communities in their turn. In this way the famous missionary centre of Lindisfarne came into existence in Northumberland. Aidan (died 651) is said to have been the first bishop, and the chronicler Bede praises him very highly. His successor Finan (died 661) carried Christianity far beyond the frontiers of Northumbria. He baptized the Angles and King Penda, the Saxon King Sigbert, and sent priests into their territories.

The Island of Iona which had the external appearance of isolation from the world remained for generations the spiritual centre, the *insula primaria* of the movement instigated by Columcille. Many monasteries founded from here preserved a constant link with Iona as *familia* of Columcille.*

Fridolin

An early Irish missionary (about 500) was Fridolt or Fridolin. Unfortunately his original biography was lost in a Hungarian raid on the monastery of Säckingen (South-West Germany) which Fridolin himself founded. Ebrard has carefully examined the sources and historical possibilities and has come to the conclusion

> ... that there was an Irishman by birth who was at first bishop in Ireland and who then in 500 came with a number of companions by way of Scotland to what was at that time the West Gothic Aquitania, that is to Poitiers (in France); here he founded a monastery and converted the bishop there and the entire population from Arianism to belief in the Trinity; he then handed the monastery over to the monks and went to France under Chlodwig and under his protection founded the monastery of St Avold in the Vosges, a church in the city of Strasburg, the monastery of Chur in Rhaetia and Säckingen in Germany. His object was the progressive conversion of the heathen. This conclusion gains additional support from the fact that the town of Glarus (old form Glaris, that is Chlaris, Hilaris†) points to the

---

* Near Iona is the small island of Staffa, with that wonder of nature, Fingal's Cave. In the steep walls of cliffs, the lower parts of which consist of columns of volcanic basalt, there is a high-roofed cave, 70 metres (230 feet) deep and about 16 metres (53 feet) high, into which the sea sends its foaming waves. The cave can be entered and in modern times the roar, surge and beat has inspired poets and musicians. To mankind still living in myth such places were revered as manifestations and marvels of the gods. The cave at Staffa must have been known to the monks of Iona. Columbanus probably spent some time on Iona or at any rate some of the monks accompanying him as missionaries knew it. When Columbanus arrived in Switzerland he is said, according to Swiss legends, to have stayed by Lake Zürich. Today there are two villages there about the same distance from each other as Iona is from Staffa. These two lakeside villages are traditionally called Iona and Staffa. This could be that Columbanus or his monks took some recollection of Iona and Staffa to the countryside around Lake Zürich.

† At Poitiers Fridolin felt the influence of St Hilary (c. 315–367). Hilary was originally a bishop in the Eastern Church who was banished to Phrygia by the Emperor Constantine who favoured the Arians. After he came to Poitiers from Phrygia, he dedicated his book *De synodis* to the 'British bishops.' Hilary therefore must have had a good relationship with the Irish movement. There was therefore already contact between Gaul and Ireland at the end of the fourth century.

founder of the Hilarius church. Also this church until 1395 was controlled by the monastery of Säckingen which indicates even more clearly a historical link with Fridolin.[9]

On the Continent

In the history of the Irish-Scottish Church and its expansion on the Continent many names are known, in historical evidence as well as in legendary accounts. Among them is the name of Brendan, who is associated with many legends. It is said that Brendan and his companions sailed the seas on voyages of adventure for many years, and possibly reached the islands of Northern and Central America. Brendan is the Odysseus of the Irish Christian missionaries.[10]

The Irishman Fursey went from eastern England, where he founded a monastery, after 630 to eastern Gaul. There he founded a monastery at Lagny near Meaux, an exercise of far-reaching influence. He died in about 650 at Mézerolles. His relics were brought to Perrone where another important Irish monastery arose. Shortly after his death his visions were written down here.

The Luxeuil monks Eustasius and Aigilus travelled to Bavaria, summoned there by Chlothar II (613–628). Rupert was active there later. Kiliam came with eleven companions from Ireland and did missionary work among the East Franks and in Thuringia, where he and two companions suffered martyrdom in 689. In Würzburg manuscripts in characteristic Irish palaeography have survived evidence of the flourishing Irish monastery there.

Corbinian as the first Bishop of Freising (Bavaria) brought Irish Christianity as far as the Southern Tyrol (now Italy), with Merano and Mais (South Merano) as centres.[11] Marianus Annianus founded the monastery at Rott on the River Inn, Bavaria.[12]

Pirminius, the founder of the famous island monastery at Reichenau (on Lake Constance), is believed to have been an Irishman.[13] A document of Theoderic IV (728) mentions him as a missionary and not as a passing Spaniard, as Jecker[14] has tried to maintain. The fragment of this text of Theoderic runs: '... the revered Pirminius, Bishop by the grace of God, is in our time here with his monks at God's command, after he had undertaken the journey to proclaim Christ ...'

The monastery of Reichenau is part of the Irish tradition. Irish monks lived there and produced a great number of valuable manuscripts. They are preserved in the Baden State Library in Karlsuhe.

The names of famous Irish missionaries and monasteries on the Continent could be increased by dozens. Here only a few points need to be made on their geographical extent. The importance of this period has been best described by Ludwig Bieler:

Recent studies of 'insular symptoms' in Continental script, illumination, and 'book technique,' of the Irish element in literature, of the give-and-take between Irish and Continental liturgy, which differs so fundamentally in attitude, have made us realise more and more that the cultural emanation from such centres as Luxeuil, Bobbio, Peronne, or the Irish-Northumbrian Echternach, must have gone far beyond the facts for which there is direct evidence, and that these centres, though of special importance, cannot have been the only points of contact between insular and Continental culture. It is hardly an exaggeration to say that between 600 and 750 AD the Irish — first alone and later together with the Anglo-Saxons — constitute the decisive cultural factor throughout the territory of the future Carolingian Empire.'[15]

14. Columbanus

With Columbanus (*c.* 540–615) a leading personality of Old Irish Christianity enters the field of vision of Continental European history. The outlines of this personality are provided by a number of reliable though fragmentary sources so that a clear picture is given of this fighter and apostle: a thoroughly Christian Occident under the guidance of the Irish Christian concept of freedom.

Columbanus (also called Columban) was born around 540 in South-East Ireland (Leinster). The first reliable biographer, the monk Jonas of Bobbio, entered the monastery of Bobbio where Columbanus had died two years before and where his memory was preserved in the immediate recollections of monks who had been his travelling companions for many years.

Jonas reports that already as a boy Columbanus, while he was still 'worldly in outlook,' eagerly studied grammar, rhetoric and written works of many kinds. This was above all possible for the sons of nobles to do at monastic schools without any intention of later becoming monks or priests. In the emotional conflicts of his youth, Columbanus turned to a 'religious woman' for counsel, and she is said to have referred to the wise Shinell at Cluainerad. It is thought that as a youthful worker guided by Shinell he wrote an interpretation of the sounds of the psalms. Ebrard mentions a few scholars who are of the opinion that the Latin commentary on the Psalms (Codex C.301), with glosses in Irish, which is preserved in the Ambrosian Library at Milan is the work of Columbanus and is in fact this youthful work.[1] In a preface the author (Columbanus?) writes that he had translated the psalms from the original Hebrew for 'those to whom he owed thanks for all that he could do.' It is reasonable to assume that Columbanus had an extensive education in languages, which included Latin, Greek and quite possible Hebrew as well.

After preparatory religious instruction under Shinell Columbanus entered the monastery of Bangor (County Down), which a little while earlier had been founded by Comgall. The range and intensity of life in this centre may be learnt from the fact that in its long heyday seven choirs with three hundred choirboys working in shifts sang and prayed 'the eternal hymns' night and day. Such customs served to give to a place a musical, mantric aura.

Virtually nothing is known of Columbanus' monastic period of more than thirty years and the many journeys which accorded with such an ebullient spirit as his, except for the legend of visiting the Island of Iona, the centre of Columcille's work. Columbanus is said to have been his pupil for a time.

Suddenly Columbanus, when nearly fifty-five years old, becomes visible to history. In 519 he decided to go on the peregrination, on a missionary journey, on the

Continent. With a band of twelve brother monks whom he had chosen — the same number as the apostles at Whitsuntide who obeyed the call to carry the Gospel to all people — he embarked and landed, probably in the southern part of Brittany or at the mouth of the Loire. The fraternal band wandered eastwards and arrived in Burgundy in about 591.

At about this time Gaul was utterly exhausted politically and religiously. The old Celtic and Roman cults had collapsed and only survived in decadent fragments. Nor at this time had the form of Christianity that could be taken seriously come from the south. It had sent no strong representative and was not in any way widespread. In view of the corruption of the ruling dynasty of the Merovingians a genuine Christian culture could not really establish itself.

In wild country on the edge of the Vosges Childebert II showed Columbanus and his companion a lonely valley where they could found an establishment. In Annegray, near present-day Luxeuil (Burgundy), literally on the ruins of the Gallic-Roman path where Attila the Hun had ravaged, Columbanus built his first monastery. Childebert was impressed by Columbanus' personality and may well have looked to the Irishman for the worldly education and training of the sons of the Frankish nobility.

The West Coast of Ireland today still retains evidence from the earliest centuries (Skellig Michael, and so on) of how monks built rectangular churches and cells with layers of stone. The appearance of these first monastic sites may well have been similar before they were expanded by the rapid arrival of students. Columbanus subsequently founded the two other sites of Luxovium (Luxeuil) and Fontaine in the neighbourhood.

The rule insisted on one solitary meal in the evening. The quiet world of monastic fraternity, scholarship and consecrated living combined with mission-ary activity in the surrounding districts soon made Luxeuil an active centre of monastic influence. The sons of noble families sought their general, worldly education here. The three monasteries — Luxeuil was the most important — expanded rapidly and the number of monks reached three hundred. On the same lines as at Bangor here, too, a day and night of 'eternal song' was instituted on a modest scale.

Columbanus' fiery, active nature was prone to adopt combative attitudes. In the imaginative language of the time his was a 'Michael nature.' Conflict with the dragon of opposition could not be postponed for long in Gaul. In particular attacks soon came from the court of the Merovingian, from Childebert's successor Theoderic II and his infamous grandmother Brunhilda, who completely dominated her grandson. There was developing antagonism therefore among the representa-tives of Gallo-Frankish Christianity, who had watched the northern version of the Irish take root in France with suspicion and repugnance.

Columbanus' plight brought about by the Gallic bishops

He loved what he believed to be the truth more than peace.

J.J. Laux on Columbanus

The Irish had a way of calculating Easter; in some years their date differed from the date of the Romans. When the Paschal Full Moon (that is, the first Full Moon after the spring equinox) was on a Sunday, in Ireland Easter was celebrated in the light of Full Moon, while the Roman Church, followed by the Gallic-Frankish Church, did so seven days later. It is remarkable that the Irish method of calculating Easter was the same roughly as that in the early Christian communities of the Eastern Church until the second century.

In AD 600 Luxeuil celebrated Easter on April 3, which was the Sunday of the Full Moon; the Frankish Church did so a week later. The Gallic clergy turned this into a charge of heresy against Columbanus. Aggressively they investigated all the other peculiarly 'Irish customs.' Columbanus lived and taught in Luxeuil. He taught liturgy, ritual, rites of baptism, and religious practices according to Irish tradition and without reference to Rome. No wonder things came to the ears of the Gallic bishops which aroused the greatest misgivings. When in the monasteries grouped round Luxeuil even the main ceremonial of the ecclesiastical year was celebrated on a different date it was thought that a concrete reason had been found for convicting the Irishman of heresy. But Columbanus had not been ordained by the Roman Church, he did not celebrate Mass and the other sacraments in the Roman manner, he ordained priests, and his actions were completely outside any Gallic-Roman jurisdiction. All these matters had roused considerable anger for some time. When the attacks of the Gallic bishops started, Columbanus wrote an intimate personal letter to Pope Gregory the Great in the conviction that the Irish tradition 'of the Early Fathers' was authentic: 'I still cannot believe that you approve of the wrong date for Easter in Gaul. I ask you: are men allowed to change what is God's as they please?'[2]

With this statement Columbanus declared himself completely in favour of the Irish calculation of the date of Easter. No answer came to him. On the contrary he was then ordered to take part in a synod of Gallic bishops at Châlon to justify himself there. Did this course seem to Columbanus to be too dangerous in view of the strength of opposition to him? Or did he see the futility of any discussion? He did not go to the synod. Instead he sent a representative there with a letter. The letter has survived. In it he said that he would not like to be guilty of ignoring the advice of St Paul to Timothy: 'Avoid such godless chatter, for it will lead people into more and more ungodliness.' (2Tim.2:16).

Meanwhile an order was issued from Rome that Columbanus was to be placed 'in the care of Abbot Conan of Lérins.' (Lérins was an island monastery off the coast of the French Riviera near Cannes.) Columbanus' letter to the Gallic synod contained an arresting call for brotherly coexistence in the deeper union with Christ.

> Permit me to be in peace and love with you and to remain in these forests, passing my life at the side of the remains of seventeen brother monks who have died ... Permit us, I beg you, to have a place beside you in Gaul ... We are all promised the same kingdom and we have one and the same hope, our faith in Christ.[3]

He went on to ask that Christ might so enlighten their hearts that because of the dispute about the date of Easter, they would not neglect the far more important evangelical duty and the care of morals. Meanwhile the Gallic bishops did not give up but tried to summon him to a synod at Arles. He answered emotionally and decisively in a letter:

> If it is God who has inspired you to drive me out of the solitude here which I looked for in my travels over land and sea, I can only say with prophet Jonah, 'Take me up and throw me into the sea: then the sea will quiet down for you; because I know that it is because of me that this great tempest has come upon you.'[4]

A wall of silence was put around Luxeuil. Columbanus had probably heard from monks travelling by that Pope Gregory had recently, in 596, sent the Roman missionary Augustine (died 604/5) to Britain with forty Benedictine monks with the aim of winning Britain to the See of Rome and bringing it under Roman jurisdiction. This Augustine did in fact succeed in doing with the help of King Ethelbert, whom he won over in establishing a Roman centre in Canterbury, whose first bishop he himself became.

The tone of Columbanus' letter becomes comprehensible against this background. He was troubled by a vision of a spiritual conflict between Celtic and Roman Christianity. Columbanus had again and again displayed a brotherly toleration or had hoped for a spiritual co-operation in striving for a common goal. Could not Celtic spirituality from the north be joined to the historical manifestation of Christ from the south in a powerful force across Europe: Ireland-Rome-Jerusalem? This idea inspired the sustained efforts of the Irish mission to the Continent and as early as the year 400 had clearly taken the initiative with Pelagius.

Columbanus' dealings with the Gallic bishops, which seemed to be reflected in the letters, aroused almost insurmountable antagonism. Is it not resignation which breaks through when he cries out in despair: 'Take me up and throw me into the sea: ... it is because of me that this great tempest has come upon you.' The task of carrying out this idea was handed over to the secular arm, the Merovingians.

Columbanus and the Merovingians

The region round Luxeuil, where Columbanus had established the centre of his work was ruled by the Merovingians. In 486 their ancestor Clovis had vowed before a decisive battle, that if he won he would follow the example of his wife and become a Christian. He won the battle and with three thousand Franks had himself baptized as a Christian in a mass baptism. But this did not have any influence on his ideas or conduct. Gregory of Tours (c. 540–594), author of the ten-volume *Historia Francorum*, reports the decadence and worldliness of Frankish Christianity. He complained of the scandalous conduct that bishops permitted themselves when it was a question of acquiring property improperly. As a result the whole of the secular power considered themselves to be released from all moral responsibility.

> Only the coarseness of the Franks and the vulgarity of the Romanized Gauls seem to be left, while the Roman culture and Germanic good nature has almost vanished. It was a time of transition in which the worst characteristics of both groups of the population were predominant. Perjury, treachery and murder of relatives were everyday occurrences.[5]

This was the 'moral atmosphere' to which Columbanus had come. Christianity could scarcely be said to exist in the land of the Franks. Theoderic II, after the violent death of his father — priests had been willing to act as hired assassins — became king while still a child. His grandmother Brunhilda who had had her own husband killed, guided and controlled the boy according to her will. Her nature can be seen in her action in having Desiderius, the Bishop of Vienne, stoned to death when he dared to criticize her conduct.

The young Theoderic II was at first attached to Columbanus, but was soon drawn by her intrigues to the side of Brunhilda. Jonas of Bobbio reports in the *Vita* of Columbanus '... then came the old serpent to his grandmother Brunhilda, who was a second Jezebel and roused her with a spur of pride against the stranger, because she saw Theoderic obeyed him.'

When Theoderic grew up and married, Brunhilda wickedly drove his young wife away in order that she might be the sole mistress of the young king. When Columbanus attempted to reunite Theoderic with the wife whom had been driven away, his action aroused Brunhilda's fear. She ordered him not to interfere and in addition demanded that by giving his blessing he should legitimize the four illegitimate children of the young king.[6] Columbanus steadfastly refused to legalize in this way the moral decadence of the court.

From now on Brunhilda was hostile to Columbanus and his Christian mission, but she found support among the Gallic bishops. In this way a plot was made to drive Columbanus out. Brunhilda seized upon the earlier dispute about the date of

Easter and the dissatisfaction of the bishops with 'Irish customs' and succeeded in forcing Theoderic to impose sanctions on the monastery at Luxeuil. The monks were forbidden to come out from the monastery walls and no one might give them shelter. An interdict was imposed on Luxeuil. Columbanus thereupon went in person to the king's residence near Autun. He remained in the courtyard and refused to enter the castle. It was said that food and drink were brought down to him and that he refused them, smashing the jug and the plate on the ground. This prophetic rage impressed Theoderic. The interdict on Luxeuil was lifted.

At this time at Brunhilda's request the Pope promoted the Bishop of Autun to the rank of archbishop and thereby strengthened the Roman headquarters against Columbanus and Luxeuil. Columbanus was a living accusation against Brunhilda. Theoderic, her tool, was to command that Columbanus abandon the 'Irish customs.' He went to Luxeuil with an army to support the demand. Columbanus prophesied his own downfall if he destroyed Luxeuil.

Theoderic turned about but ordered an official of his court to arrest Columbanus. In 610 he was seized by force and confined in the fortress of Besançon. He was allowed one monk to attend him. Imprisoned here he was to await the king's further orders.

It is not known how many weeks or months this imprisonment lasted. Columbanus decided to escape. His spiritual mission permitted him to defy arbitrary worldly power. Did he really act as his biographer Jonas of Bobbio reports? His version is that when Columbanus' return to Luxeuil became known the furious Theoderic appeared at the monastery there with the intention of piercing the insubordinate man with his own spear. Then he describes how Columbanus came to meet him and how the spear fell from his hand. Theoderic fell at the feet of the abbot, 'troubled by an evil spirit.' For many days Columbanus cared for the deranged king in the monastery, 'prayed for him and with him,' and in this way healed him.

The attack launched by Brunhilda with the support of the Frankish bishops did not cease. A royal decree was issued ordering Columbanus to return to Ireland together with all those who had come from Ireland with him. Melodrama of courage, steadfastness and submission to destiny lay behind the proceedings of his renewed arrest. The royal escort was entrusted with the duty of conducting Columbanus and the Irish monks who had entered the country with him twenty years ago down the River Loire to Nantes, and putting them on board a ship bound for Ireland. And this was done. In Tours Columbanus was allowed to visit the grave of St Martin.

The most significant dialogues of world history are nowhere recorded. Before Columbanus embarked he wrote to the monks of Luxeuil and to Attala, his favourite pupil, whom he appointed abbot, a farewell letter, evidence of his agitated state of mind. Here is an excerpt:

To his beloved sons and pupils, his brothers in simple living ...

Peace be with you — and eternal love!

Only God knows how troubled I am about your well-being and how gladly I should like to see you progressing in sacred knowledge ...

You know the struggle was not undertaken for the sake of ephemeral things, but for the Kingdom of Heaven — a struggle which is in no way a new one. Men persecute you but do not do so freely ... evil spirits are in them, who envy you your spiritual wealth; take up the arms of God against them and with the arrows of zealous prayer open up your path to heaven ...

I feel that the dispute concerning Easter will break out again and that our enemies will send you away if you do not conform; as I am no longer with you they will believe that you will no longer resist them ...

[Addressed to Attala]:

You have learned from my fate ... men's characters are very varied; this variety you will bear in mind, and you will vary your own self for the benefit of those who have shown you love and loyalty ...

I wanted initially, dear Attala, to write you a letter full of grief and tears. But when I considered that in any case your own heart sighs under the burden of worries and cares, I changed the tone ... and kept all the pain buried deep in my soul ...

So let us climb up the royal path of crucifixion of the flesh and the heart's penitence ... by the grace of God, by faith, hope and love ...

Never fear the battle, do not fail to recognize your powerful enemy or forget the freedom which your rule possesses. There is no struggle where there is no adversary, and no victory where there is no struggle, and where no freedom is there is no honour.

As I write news is brought to me that the ship in which against my will I am to be carried back to my homeland lies ready to depart ...

My parchment forces me to finish this letter, though the wealth of my material demands yet more space. Love knows nothing of system that is why my writing is confused ... Pray for me, sons of my heart, so that I may live in God.[7]

The forced embarkation on a 'Scottish trading vessel' took place in Nantes. Jonas relates that when the ship was about to gain the open sea it was driven back on the shore by the wind and the waves. After three days, the ship's captain gave permission for Columbanus and the monks to leave the vessel. He could not return to Luxeuil and therefore chose a more northerly route by way of Paris and reached the court of King Chlotar II of Neustria, who was favourably disposed to him. Columbanus left his brilliant pupil Potentiums with him to found a monastery in the region according to the rule of Luxeuil.[8]

From here he journeyed on to the city of Metz, where the court of King Theudebert of Austrasia was established. This man, the brother of the evil Theoderic, who had driven Columbanus out, was at this time preparing for war against his brother. His reception of Columbanus was therefore cordial in the extreme. He soon formed a tie of friendship with Chagmerich, the king's principal adviser. One of his sons came as a pupil to Columbanus. From this brief visit in Metz monasteries are said to have been founded in the district. From Luxeuil a number of monks came to join Columbanus. Among them was Attala, who was still especially devoted to him. King Theudebert invited Columbanus to select a region in his kingdom for a centre for his work. The Lake of Constance was chosen, but at that time was more or less pagan. Here were openings for missionary work which led to Southern Germany, to Helvetia, to Austria and the Danube countries.

King Theudebert placed a rowing boat with a crew of retainers at the disposal of the seventy-year-old Columbanus. It would take him and his companions down the Moselle and then up the Rhine to Basle. There is a tradition that Columbanus composed a boatman's song, and that he and his companions sang this in time with the rhythm of the oars. The original text survives in Latin.[9] The journey up the Rhine, the harshness of the weather, the defiance of the storm and rocks are all made in this lyrical hymn a metaphor for the journey of life and its struggles.

See, cut in wood, through flood of twin-horned Rhine
passes the keel, and greased slips over seas —
Heave, men! And let resounding echo sound our 'heave.'

The winds raise blasts, wild rain-storms wreak their spite
but ready strength of men subdues it all —
Heave, men! And let resounding echo sound our 'heave.'

Clouds melt away and the harsh tempest stills,
effort tames all, great toil is conqueror —
Heave, men! And let resounding echo sound our 'heave.'

Endure and keep yourselves for happy things;
ye suffered worse, and these too God shall end —
Heave, men! And let resounding echo sound our 'heave.'

Thus acts the foul fiend: wearing out the heart
and with temptation shaking inmost parts —
Ye men, remember Christ with mind still sounding 'heave.'

Stand firm in soul and spurn the foul fiend's tricks
and seek defence in virtue's armoury —
Ye men, remember Christ with mind still sounding 'heave.'

Firm faith will conquer all and blessed zeal
and the old fiend yielding breaks at last his darts —
Ye men, remember Christ with mind still sounding 'heave.'

Supreme, of virtues King, and fount of things,
He promises in strife, gives prize in victory —
Ye men, remember Christ with mind still sounding 'heave.'

It is thought that Columbanus and his companions left the ship in the neighbourhood of Basle.

On Lake Constance

Among the companions of Columbanus who came with him to Lake Constance are men named Attala, Gallus, Eustasius and Sigisbert. They came across traces of Celtic Christianity. Fridolin had had influence on the Rhine, a certain Willimar was mentioned in Arbon, who received Columbanus as a brother. The population was for the most part still heathen. Columbanus started to establish a new centre of his activities at Bregenz. But only three years were granted him to work here; then came the terrible news that Theudebert, his royal protector and ruler of the Lake Constance region, had been killed in a battle with his brother Theoderic. This resulted in all Austrasia, which included the upper Rhine region, coming into the power of Brunhilda, the arch-enemy of Columbanus. It was impossible for him to stay any longer, and he decided to go on with a few companions southwards into Italy. It is clear that in his last years he still wanted to build the axis Ireland-Rome, as a bridge of Christian understanding.*

On his journey up the Rhine with only a few companions, Columbanus left Sigisbert behind in the district of the source of the Rhine. This monk founded the monastery at Disentis which flourished later.[10] It is possible that Columbanus, now more than seventy years old, climbed over the Lukmanier Pass, which leads from

---

* Jonas of Bobbio makes no mention of Gallus disobediently remaining by the Lake of Constance and being barred from celebrating Mass as a punishment. It can only be said of this strange legend (possibly of a later date) that Columbanus did not celebrate the Roman Mass at all. The Irish had their own ritual forms. Columbanus cannot be blamed for imposing a spiritual sanction on a fellow monk, one who had taken it upon himself to continue fulfilling a difficult duty from which later developed the flourishing life of the Irish monastery of St Gallen.

Disentis to Olivone. A little way above Olivone towards the Lukmanier Pass there still stands an ancient church over whose entrance there is an inscription on the wall: San Colombano. This Columbanus church appears to be a memorial of his journey over the Lukmanier Pass.

Columbanus in Italy

When the difficulty of crossing the Alps in those days is considered, it is clear that a particular impulse must have been behind the Italian journey of the now elderly Columbanus. Attala, his favourite follower, whom he had chosen at Luxeuil, was with him and probably other companions. In 613 they arrived at the court at Milan of the Lombard King Agilulf, an Arian Christian. His wife, Theudelinde, had been a friend of Pope Gregory the Great and a Roman Catholic. At Milan Columbanus was received 'with honour' by the king, and received his help and protection. He allotted a district in the Apennines to Columbanus where he could found a monastery. Jonas says of this:

> At this time a man by the name of Jocundus appeared before the king and reported to him that he knew a church of the holy Apostle Peter in a very lonely place in the Apennines. The place had many like this. It was unusually fertile and the streams were full of fish. It had from ancient times been called Bobium, after the river flowing past. Another river was called Trebbia, and beside it Hannabel had once spent the winter. Thither now went Columbanus and with great effort restored the church, which had partly collapsed, in all its former beauty and constructed whatever else was needed for a monastery.

Agilulf did in fact hand a considerable gift to Columbanus in the Trebbia Valley. An inscription records the deed: King Agilulf 'gives the worthy Columbanus and his companion the basilica of the Holy Prince of Apostles at Bobbio, and with it surrounding land in a radius of four miles ... As a return for the king's generosity the monks are to pray to God daily for the support and prosperity of the realm.'[11]

Once more Columbanus worked at building, this time at the most southern of the Celtic monasteries, as Jonas describes it. In the neighbourhood of Bobbio two grottoes are pointed out, where Columbanus is said to have withdrawn at times to meditate. From the Bobbio period a most unusual but inconsistently contradictory letter to Pope Boniface IV is attributed to Columbanus. On the one hand this is full of expressions of quite untypical servile subservience, while on the other hand it addresses its distinguished recipient in polemical, blustering tones. Hardly any historians consider it to be genuine. The thorough Delius ignores it completely, Jonas of Bobbio knows nothing of it. It is not intended to go into this question here, but it

Figure 119. The sarcophagus of Columbanus, at Bobbio, Italy.

should not be forgotten that this strange document is conveniently used to illustrate Columbanus' submission to the See of Rome. Later Columbanus, long after his death, was declared to be a saint by the Roman Church and was worshipped as one.

It is true that for Columbanus Rome was a sacred place because of the martyrdom of Peter and Paul. But how independent his attitude to the See of Rome was is shown by the genuine letter to Pope Gregory.

Meanwhile in France the gruesome royal struggle reached some sort of conclusion when in 613 Theoderic, Columbanus' opponent, was brutally slaughtered together with his sons and Brunhilda by Chlotar II. Chlotar now became sole Merovingian king. He sent the Luxeuil monk Eustasius as envoy to Bobbio to tell Columbanus that he could return as Abbot to Luxeuil. Columbanus declined. Jonas reports his answer: '... it was not God's will that he should climb across the Alps again.'

The same Eustasius afterwards became Abbot at Luxeuil, when he returned from Bobbio with Columbanus' blessing. Columbanus lived on in Bobbio for nearly two years, and died there on November 23, 625. His remains still rest today in the crypt there as 'San Colombano.' His faithful pupil Attala succeeded him as abbot.

An aptly symbolic legend recounts that Columbanus' pilgrim staff was by his will brought to Gallus who had remained at the Lake of Constance. The monastery of St Gallen developed thereafter as a Celtic centre which radiated great influence. But the figure of Columbanus as the unyielding militant apostle looms full of significance long after his own century.

Despite the great distance from Ireland, Bobbio kept in contact with Mother Ireland and the monastery of Bangor from which Columbanus had come. Important Irish manuscripts came to the library of this Apennine monastery. Attala also maintained contact with Luxeuil. He returned to Bobbio from a journey there with the Luxeuil monk Bertulf, who later became his successor (627–664).

The 'Monastic Rule'

In the seventh and eighth centuries a 'Monastic Rule' of Columbanus was widely used in the Celtic monasteries on the Continent. It is natural to expect that as a result of this, important evidence would be obtainable concerning the personal life in the monasteries as an aspect of Columban spirituality. For various reasons this is not the case. It is true that four hand-written documents exist, of which the oldest and most trustworthy comes from Bobbio. This one, as well as one from St Gallen, was written *after* Columbanus' death. His pupil Donat, later Bishop of Vesontio, issued a few decades after Columbanus' death a *Regulo Columbani* which, however, was a mixture and already contained a lot of Benedictine material. The other records (at the Benedictine Abbey at Ochsenhausen and the Benedictine Monastery at Augsburg) differ greatly from the Bobbio texts and expand a Book of Penitance which wrongly uses Columbanus' name in connection with the practice of torture.[12]

If the characteristics of the rule that came into existence at Bobbio after Columbanus' death are studied, the strict spiritual training is most impressive. This was imposed on the monks in order that they might overcome human failings. The sanctification of life is throughout the ideal perfection which an able individual monk can, to a greater or lesser extent, approach by training. The monk is to become a part of God's kingdom and represent and reveal it on this earth. Since there were no externally imposed hierarchical grades as in an organized Church, authority was vested only in the inner worth and example of the leaders, of the 'elders,' of the abbots and bishops. The way the human can be purified and imbued with the divine by inner discipline is the goal of this rule. Here are a few of the main ideas of the oldest rules, which are again stressed in the headings of the individual rules.

1. *On obedience.* Obedience even against the will is a way to humility and a readiness to serve.
2. *On the duty of silence.* 'For by your words you will be justified, and by your words you will be condemned' (Matt.12:37). The tongue must be guided by reason.
3. *On temperance.* The diet is to be vegetarian and light 'so that the body is

not overburdened and the spirit not choked.' Intelligence demands that spiritual progress be assisted by restraint in the satisfaction of sensual desires.

4. *On poverty.* Those who each day follow Christ have their treasure in heaven; on earth they must be content with the bare necessities. Giving up possessions is the first step towards perfection; the second step is purification of the heart, the third (and highest) step though is the unceasing love of God and heavenly things.

5. *On overcoming vanity.* Pleasure in oneself is dangerous. Let the monk never utter a boasting word.

6. *On chastity.* What is bodily virginity worth, if it is not also present in the spirit?

7. *On wisdom.* Wisdom (*discretio*) is the ability to distinguish between good and evil, between mediocre and the excellent. The prime evil is pride, and its opposite is humility. From these two roots a forest of opposites has grown.

8. *On mortifying the will.* Mortification of the self is indeed intolerable to the proud and inflexible, and a great solace to the meek. For them is the saying: '... not as I will, but as thou wilt' (Matt. 26:39).

9. *On perfection.* The monk is to live in the monastery in company with many others and in obedience to a father in order to learn humility from him, and patience from the others. To learn the doctrine of silence from the one, and to receive the doctrine of meekness from the others.[13]

The monastic rule of Columbanus was not a monastery of statute or coded duties. It was rather a paternal and insistent question and challenge: 'How does one achieve an ever more consummate life, knowing that supersensory realities are a fact, so as to be able to take part in the task of the redemption of mankind?' This requires the training of the self, a personal striving and a struggle to overcome the 'sinful part' in mankind and to transform it. The Rule does not mention administration, and official authorities. Everything here seems to rest on human qualities and on the spiritual authority of the abbot. Consequently penances for shortcomings can be decided individually from case to case and in this way atonement was sensibly made for impure thoughts, intentions or actions, and in this way could be experienced in anticipation the purification after death of purgatory, which was so impressively described in the visions of the Irishman Fursas of Munster.[14] The fact that Columbanus practised a system of penances without fixed penitential rules and code of punishment is clearly in accord with his kind of spirituality and with the oldest Irish tradition.

If in the centuries following Columbanus' death books on penances appear which bear his name, the probable explanation is that examples were taken from penances in practice and reduced to fixed punishment rules. Subsequently these were quite arbitrarily expanded and changed. But his name, with its great prestige, was quite unscrupulously used to foist matters on him with which he had no longer anything to do. Only in this way can the flogging code be judged which was called 'Columbanus' Punishment Book.'[15] In this, for small, harmless 'offences,' shocking sentences of flogging were imposed on monks. Here are some examples: anyone who does not make the sign of the cross on the spoon before eating with it shall receive eight lashes. Anyone who does not say amen at the end of a meal, thirty lashes. Anyone who coughs when singing Psalms, six lashes. Anyone who talks to a layman must sing twenty-four punishment Psalms, and so on. The idea of beating in a Christian way of living with the knout and associating this practice with the name of Columbanus could only arise in a period in which the memory of the Irish Christian movement was being deliberately discredited. These so-called 'Columbanus Rules' breathe an alien spirit. What did he say in his farewell letter to his pupils and followers in Luxeuil?

> Seeking to preserve everything firmly in accordance with the Rule I endeavoured to join all the weak branches to the roots of the tree ...
> You are to consider carefully the different qualities of each individual, and to take into account the differences of character which are so marked among human beings. You will understand how to make yourselves vary ....'[16]

This tender exposition of human individuality, which was typical of Columbanus was characteristic of the Celts. Penance on the path of asceticism and training of the self was not in Columbanus' view a means of striving egotistically for personal salvation, but helped to make the soul open to the passage of 'divine things.' As a result the power to preach and prophesy should develop. The way to the inner self could help to prepare the way to the outer world.

15. Missionaries in Switzerland

When Columbanus and a number of his companions travelled up the Rhine there is an old tradition that his pupil Ursicinus (probably with one companion) parted from him at Basle and travelled to Lake Biel.[1] Here he established a Christian community. In later years he made his way to the upper Doubs region and founded a monastery, today the monastery of St Ursanne (Canton Jura).

Halfway between Biel and Geneva is the site of one of the earliest monastic foundations of Roman Christianity in Switzerland. It is Romainmôtier, founded around 400 by Roman of Condat. In the first half of the seventh century a colony of Irish monks led by Ramelenus settled here. This monk was the son of Duke Aldenenus (Waldenenus) of Besançon, who had formed a close friendship with Columbanus at Luxeuil. It is thought that the small Roman Christian monastic society had become so reduced in numbers that the Irish monks were welcome. This would be a rare example of fraternal unity of north and south. From the beginning of the eighth century this monastery was regarded as a Celtic one. To this day an ancient stone pulpit has survived with its beautiful Lombard stonework and sun cross. As part of the subsequent expansion of the Roman Church and restriction of Irish Christianity no less a person than Pope Stephen III passed here on a journey in 753 to consecrate a new church building in person. Only after that was the monastery called *Roman*-Môtier, or Romainmôtier, and made subordinate to Rome.

In connection with this is the tradition of an Irish Christianizing in the Bernese Oberland spreading from the area around the Lake of Thun by means of the missionaries Beatus and Justus.[2] According to the legends these two wandered from northern Switzerland, past Lake Zug, through Unterwalden and over the Brünig Pass into the Bernese Oberland. The artist lived in a cave by the Lake of Thun, and here the legendary fight with a dragon took place (symbol of the Michaelic Christian warrior spirit). The mountain with the Beatus Cave still has the name today of Beatenberg.

It is not improbable although it cannot be proved that Beatus and Justus have some connection with Columbanus' disciples. Beatus was a name frequently chosen for Irish itinerant monks and missionaries. It is remarkable that the names Sankt Batt (or Pat) and Battenberg (found on old maps) have tenaciously survived by the Lake of Thun into the twentieth century. A link with the name of Patrick is also possible. Beatus could then be the medieval Latin form of Batt, as it was customary in those days to use a Latin name which sounded similar.

The valley adjacent to the Beatenberg is called Justistal, where according to legend Justus lived in a hermit's cell and brought Christianity into Emmental. In 1904 a rock grave was discovered in the course of excavation in Beatus Cave, which had been a famous object of pilgrimage in the Middle Ages. At the time of the Reformation the Berne government ordered the cave to be closed by a thick wall to put a stop to the pilgrimages. Chroniclers report that the relics of Beatus were taken from the grave and quickly buried in the nearby village.

It is worthy of note that in the course of renovation and excavation by the Lake of Thun in Spiez, Einigen, Faulensee and Leissigen, very old foundations of churches were discovered which were dated as seventh century. This was the time of the influence of Columbanus and his pupils in Switzerland. These foundations have the rectangular form characteristic of old Irish churches, while the apse came from the south. Only in a few cases was there any difficulty in determining whether the weak curve of the apse came from a later period. These surprising discoveries of recent decades were in agreement with the fact that the original small church at Faulensee bore the name 'Columban-Kapelle' until it became a ruin in the last century.

The Lake of Thun neighbourhood and the districts to the north of it belonged to the See of Constance until the early Middle Ages. The See of Constance was connected with the Irish tradition. The more southern districts belong to the See of Lausanne, a Roman Catholic centre. If all these matters are taken into consideration the Irish mission by the Lake of Thun can be held to be historically true. The Lake of Thun established a kind of spiritual frontier between Roman and Irish Christianity until the eighth century. This frontier extended west into the Jura (the most southern point Romainmôtier) and eastwards over the watershed into the direction of Grisons (Disentis) and on into Austria and to the Danube. Even Vienna had its 'Scottish Monastery.' Mention has already been made of the Irish Mission in the Southern Tyrol.

After Columbanus' death

After Columbanus' death Eustasius was abbot of Luxeuil. This monastery continued to flourish and at this time had six hundred monks. Eustasius was soon slanderously accused by Agrestin, a former monk, of unchristian beliefs and heresy.

Jonas of Bobbio says about this:

> At the king's orders, a large number of Burgundian Bishops met in the outskirts of Macon ... Warnachaire, who was the enemy of the blessed Eustasius ... was starting his speech against Eustasius, [when] he was suddenly struck down dead. This even threw Agrestin's party into a state of panic; the latter was pressed to make a personal attack on Columban's Rule and on the venerable Eustasius. Agrestin, however, started to tremble, for he had no gift of oratory and was unable to make himself heard with authority; he was only able to make foolish remarks ... then, combining impudence with false charges, he started to criticize their special form of

tonsure and their particular way of writing, in short the different way of life which they followed ... Eustasius, having given proof of his impatience, then allowed his wisdom to shine out and exclaimed with relevance: 'In the presence of these priests,' he said, 'I, the disciple and successor of him whose discipline and rule you now attack, summon you to appear, before the end of the year, at the Divine Tribunal, where you shall discuss these matters with him: you will then receive punishment from the most just Judge, for with lying talk you have attempted to tarnish the reputation of his servant.' When they heard these words, all those who up to then had been Agrestin's supporters were troubled in their souls, and they all asked that an agreement should be reached ... Eustasius showed his gentleness and strength of soul, for he yielded to the general entreaty, agreed to peace, and gave the kiss of reconcilation.[3]

Eustasius agreed to a compromise, and made the date of Easter agree with the Roman date. Because of this action by Eustasius Luxeuil was once more successfully kept free from the Gallic Church and able to continue to cultivate the Irish tradition.

At Bobbio Bertulf became abbot after the death of Columbanus' pupil Attala. Here too hostile action by nearby monasteries and bishoprics developed. Consequently Bertulf went direct to Pope Honorius at Rome. He told him about the life and cares of the monastery at Bobbio. Jonas reports that Honorius was very gentle and showed great understanding. He was willing to grant the monastery at Bobbio a special statute: 'You wish this monastery to come under the jurisdiction of no priest of another church and be subordinate to no other authority than the direct authority of the Pope ... As a result of Bertulf's action the first compromise was made with the Roman Church. Bobbio was released from the jurisdiction of the Tortona diocese and this was the first papal grant of privileged exemption in the Western Church.[4] For Bobbio this brought the certain freedom from the attacks it had endured, though in the end it resulted in complete Romanization. In 643, two years after Bertulf's death, Bobbio was committed to the Benedictine Rule. The last privileges expired in the tenth century.

If these events are considered in conjunction with the struggle of Eustasius at Luxeuil it is clear that immediately after Columbanus' death Rome's efforts made progress towards the goal of making all Western Christianity subordinate to a single Church. The struggle to achieve this in the British Isles was conducted from Canterbury. It was only a question of time before this was achieved by forceful means.

16. The Dispute Between Rome and Ireland

Irish Christianity had a consciousness of missionary duty that had begun already in the fifth century with its spread to Britain and the Continent. As the Roman Church made more and more claims to universality, defections to the free forms of old Irish Christianity occasioned acute crises. This was particularly the case whenever the two tendencies encountered each other working in the same region. At first the Irish missionary Pelagius had made great impact on Southern Europe. As a result a number of different measures and actions can be distinguished by which the Roman Church attempted to integrate Irish Christianity into its organization. It was decided at the Gallic synod in 429 to send Bishop Germanus and Bishop Lupus to Britain to combat Pelagianism (see p.166). This missionary delegation made its way towards Scotland, but nothing is known of its subsequent activity.

A little later, according to the account of the contemporary chronicler Prosper of Aquitaine, Pope Celestine I sent Bishop Palladius 'to the Irish believing in Christ.' Bieler makes this comment: 'The task of Palladius might have been limited ... He might have come not as a missionary, but merely as an organizer ...'[1] In other words he tried to Romanize the Old Irish Christianity and incorporate it into the Roman Church. In this case, too, nothing is known of the result of the mission except Prosper's report that Palladius died just a year later. Prosper notwithstanding continues in the style of a tendentious chronicler:

> Pope Celestine was very severe against the promoters of Pelagianism. He delivered the British lands from this disease with much zeal; there were enemies of Grace living in those places where it had its origin; he even drove them out of the most distant areas into the ocean.[2]

In this way the two earliest known attempts at Romanization came to nothing. Only around the year 600 did the Roman Church, under Gregory I, first gain a foothold in England.

Gregory I, the mission to the Angles

When Pope Gregory I, known as Gregory the Great, took over the See of Rome in 590, he wrote as follows to the Patriarch John of Constantinople: 'Unworthy and weak as I am, I have taken over an old ship, much damaged by the waves. The water pours in on every side, and its rotten timbers, beaten daily by continual storms, proclaim with their moans shipwreck and sinking.'

Above all others the Germanic people with the fresh vigour of youth carried war

and destruction through the declining Roman Empire. While Gregory's predecessors had paid attention to the Orient and the Occident, Gregory turned his attention
towards the North, towards the Germanic peoples. In this connection the missionary work among the Anglo-Saxons constitutes his most momentous decision that
affected Irish Christianity. E. Caspar calls this initiative 'the most important event in
Papal history for many years.'[3] A year after Gregory's election as Pope, Columbanus
and his twelve companions were on the Continent and had already founded the
Luxeuil centre in Gaul. Obviously Gregory had got wind of this Irish 'invasion.' The
Roman bishops of Gaul likewise turned against Columbanus, and as a result
Columbanus himself wrote direct to Pope Gregory.

As early as September 595 Gregory wrote to the presbyter Candidus on his taking
over the patrimony of Gaul and gave him the task of using ecclesiastical money to
buy Anglo-Saxon boys in the slave markets of Gaul with the object of training them
in Roman monasteries 'so that they might be dedicated to the service of Almighty
God.'[4] The mission to the Angles was therefore a long-term project concerned with
future generations.

In Columbanus' fifth year of work at Luxeuil came Gregory's countermove. In the
summer of 596 forty Benedictine monks under the leadership of Augustine left
Rome and set out through Gaul on their way to Britain. These Benedictine monks
came from Gregory's own monastery of St Andrew on the Clivus Scauri in Rome.

On this journey it is thought that the large delegation spent the winter at Autun.[5]
Here Augustine, at Gregory's request, was ordained bishop by Bishop Syagaris. It
was therefore in the district where Columbanus worked that the dedication of a
bishop was proclaimed for Rome's mission to Britain, probably with support from
the Merovingian court.

In the autumn of 596 the forty Benedictine monks trod on the soil of southern
England, bringing a silver Roman cross, icons (pictures of saints on a wooden
base), ritual garments and relics and gifts for King Ethelbert and his wife. She was
Brunhilda's niece, a Frankish princess, and an adherent of the Gallo-Roman
Church. The letter from Pope Gregory which Augustine handed to King Ethelbert
has survived: 'We are sending you small gifts but they will not seem small to you
when you realize that they bring you the blessing of the holy apostle Peter ... Above
all listen to Augustine. The more faithfully you fulfil what he in God's stead says to
you the sooner will God himself hear him when he prays for you.'[6] Augustine gained
the favour of the ruling pair. He established a centre at Canterbury and there
became the first Roman metropolitan in Britain.

In July 598 Gregory reported in a letter that survives that at Christmas (597) more
than ten thousand Anglo-Saxons were baptized by Augustine. It is improbable that
so many 'heathens' could be converted to Christianity in a few months. It is conceivably a case of rebaptizing Celtic Christians into the Roman Church. Tradition
reveals no clear explanation.

Augustine began in Britain with mass baptism whereas the Irish way was that the individual would be gradually guided to spiritual maturity as a Christian and only then baptized. Augustine used the baptism as a means of obtaining and reporting to Rome as many Church members as possible. Gregory in his letters expressed his joy at the 'successful conversions' of the Anglo-Saxons. Augustine was made an Archbishop and was instructed to create two metropolitan sees at London and York, each with twelve bishoprics. The organization of the Roman Church made rapid progress.

Bede recounts that King Ethelbert organized a synod at 'Augustine's oak' at which both the Benedictine monks and Irish priests were present.[7] The Roman Christians demanded that the Irish abandon their own special customs. No agreement was reached, but a second, larger synod followed, in which a number of Irish bishops and scholars from Bangor (North Wales) took part. Augustine demanded that they give up the Irish date of Easter, adopt the Roman baptismal rite and acknowledge himself as archbishop. The Irish declined to do so. They said to themselves: 'Nay, if he will not so much as rise to us, how much the more, if we now begin to subject ourselves to him, will he hereafter despise us and set us at nought.' Even the chronicler Bede, himself friendly to Rome, describes Augustine and his attitude to the old British (Celtic) Church as 'arrogant and ill-tempered.'[8] So the two Christian movements remained divided into two camps. The North still remained attached to Irish Christianity.

The Synod of Whitby

The influence of Columcille's mission and the monks of Iona still flourished in north England. From the centre at Lindisfarne its founder, Bishop Aidan (died 651) spread its influence and for many decades he remained the much esteemed leader of Celtic Christianity. As a result of the help of the royal house (Ethelbert) and increasing missionary activity and rebaptism, southern England had almost entirely gone over to the Roman confession. Oswald, king of Northumbria, had prompted the foundation of Lindisfarne by Aidan and remained a friend of the abbot. The king accompanied him on missionary expeditions among his own people, particularly at the beginning of Aidan's work. He translated his words into Anglo-Saxon, as Aidan had not yet mastered the local language. In this way Celtic Christianity spread from Iona through Northumbria. Only after the death of Aidan and King Oswald did Roman Christianity begin to push up from the south. King Oswald's son and successor was Oswy, who had been educated by Wilfrid, a Lindisfarne monk.[9]

Whether as a result of approaches from Benedictine circles, or on some other ground, this Wilfrid travelled to Rome and there accepted the Roman practices completely. On his way back he spent three years in the monastery at Lyons. When

Wilfrid returned to Northumbria King Oswy appointed him as tutor of Crown Prince Egfrid. Wilfrid, originally a Celtic monk, now started to work against this form of Christianity and taught the crown prince accordingly. In the same way he had influence on the second prince, Alfrid, whom Oswy appointed as Viceroy of Deiria. It is reported of him that he took a monastery away from the Celts because they would not agree to Wilfrid's Roman observance. Shortly afterwards Wilfrid strongly supported the organization of a synod between representatives of the Celtic and of the Roman Church. It was to be held at Whitby. The main item of discussion was to be the diverging calculation of the date of Easter by the Celtic and the Roman Church.

This dispute is known as the Paschal Controversies. It is a complex and difficult question, as traditions varied.[10] The conflict basically concerns a superficial symptom of a deeper, spiritual difference. According to surviving traditional accounts these spiritual differences did not come to open discussion.

Here is the place for a brief attempt to explain the dispute. The date of Easter is determined by the first Full Moon after the spring equinox, the 'Paschal Moon.' There are different methods of cyclical calculations to determine the future date of a Paschal Moon. The Church of Asia Minor, following John the Evangelist, celebrated Easter on whatever day of the week the Paschal Moon fell. The other Churches celebrated Easter on Sundays. The main difference between the Celtic and the Roman method arose if the Paschal Moon fell on a Sunday. The Celtic Church celebrated Easter on that Sunday, while the Roman Easter was a week later.

Pope Hilarus introduced a variant on this cycle in 465, and this underwent a further alteration in the method of calculation in 525. The Synod of Arles in Columbanus' time declared: 'Whoever does not celebrate Easter with Rome does not eat the body of the Lamb, but the dragons' meat ....'[11] This is taken from a letter of an Irish monk Cummianus, who had been converted in Rome. It was written in 650 to the Abbot of Iona. The letter continued, 'Rome is supported by the whole world against the Scots,' and rhetorically denounces, 'this handful of Britons and Scots in the remotest corner of the world.' He describes them as heretical deviants.

Against this view the Irish pointed to a variety of revisions carried out by the Roman Church. They themselves considered they had the duty of preserving the original Christian tradition. Until 465 the method of calculating used by the Celtic and the Eastern Church had not been condemned. Only when the Celtic and Roman Church met in Columbanus' time was this difference branded as an incriminating antagonism. It was an *outer sign* of the refusal of Old Irish Christianity to become subordinate to Rome.

At the Synod of Whitby in 664 a decision was to be made whether the Irish monks might legitimately continue their activities in Northumbria or must submit to the Roman practices — first of all in the matter of the celebration of Easter. This kingdom of Oswy was the last Anglo-Saxon realm where the Scots had not been driven out by Rome's representatives. Bede gives a very full report of the proceedings at the synod. The main representative of the Celtic side was Colman, Abbot of Lindisfarne, accompanied by Gedda, Abbot of Lestingham, and Hulda, Abbess of Whitby. The Roman view was represented by Wilfrid.

King Oswy opened the synod with a speech in which he asserted that whoever served God in any way must also conform to a rule concerning Easter.

Colman explained that he had received his method of observing Easter from a higher source which could be traced back to the Evangelist John, the disciple whom the Lord loved. This could not be despised or rejected.

Opposing this Wilfrid pointed to the greatness and authority of the Church in Rome. The Irish calculation of Easter was stupid, foolish work (*stultus labor*). He stressed the authority of Peter. In Rome Easter was celebrated *after* the Paschal Moon. John had, indeed, celebrated it with the Jews on the Paschal Moon but after his death this had been changed in Asia Minor. They (the Celts) agreed with neither John nor Peter. Columba and the Irish Fathers had indeed erred from ignorance. And then Wilfrid cried out: 'What is Columba compared with Peter!' He quoted Christ's words: 'You are Peter, and on this rock will I build my church' (Matt. 16:18).

King Oswy then joined in and asked Colman 'Did Christ really say that?'

Colman: 'Yes, Oswy.'

Oswy: 'Can you bring forward any special authority given your Columba?'

Colman: 'No, Oswy.'

'Then I shall obey him who has the power to open and shut heaven.'

And so in the king's dominions the synod had decided in favour of Rome.

Colman soon after left the country with a 'bleeding heart,' taking with him the relics of Aidan, the founder of Lindisfarne, on his return to the north. Wilfrid was installed as Bishop of Northumbria, and introduced the Roman ritual and Latin as the language of the Church. At the Council of Hertford in 673 Egfrid, Oswy's second son, Viceroy of York, had to restrain the fanatical zeal of Wilfrid; as Wilfrid was unwilling to accept this restraint, Egrid dismissed and banished him in 678.[12] He appointed more moderate successors.

After Egfrid's death Wilfrid returned from a long visit to Rome and with Rome's blessing regained the See of York. Shortly afterwards he died in 709. As a result a kind of coexistence between the rival Churches continued in Northumbria for some time.

Symptomatic of these contradictions was the personality of the Abbot Adamnan of Iona. In the course of a journey around Northumbria in 684 he was won over to support the Roman Easter and tonsure. On his return to Iona he tried to persuade his brother monks to share his view. He met with strong resistance and felt himself obliged to leave Iona. He went to South Ireland, where Romanization had also established a foothold. Was Adamnan disappointed here and did he again feel obliged to leave? Later he made his way back to Iona and died there in 704.

In conclusion it can be established that the mission to the Angles of Gregory the Great was, from Rome's point of view, successfully advancing along the road to establishing a uniform, Western Church. From the viewpoint of Old Irish Christianity it resulted in a degree of human tragedy that cannot be measured historically. The Synod of Whitby was a small, typical portion of a far more widespread process which occurred not only in the British Isles, but achieved its ends above all on the Continent in the eighth century. The destruction of the free Celtic movement was its objective. Boniface was the key figure in this action.

17. Boniface and the Destruction of the Celtic Church in Germany

A century after Columbanus, Boniface (675–754), an Anglo-Saxon, developed his activities on the Continent, but under a different banner. He, too, worked steadfastly and untiringly. He has been called the 'Apostle of the Germans' by historians not entirely free from bias. Detailed knowledge of his work reveals that he was less a 'converter of the heathen' than a commissioner with the task of bringing into the Roman Church those regions on the mainland which had been Christianized by the Irish and the Scots. Boniface was to have the task and fate of doing on the Continent what Wilfrid had done in England. The story of his life is also an account of excessive repression and destruction of the Celtic movement and the achievement of total Romanization in northern Europe, above all in Germany.

His Anglo-Saxon name was originally Wynfrith. He was born about 675 at Crediton in Wessex and was educated, it is thought, in the monastery at Exeter.

It is known that he was subsequently for some time at the Nursling Monastery between Southampton and Winchester. There, in 710 he was ordained as priest. When he was forty he went to Frisia (Holland), where the Celt Willibrord and his companions had been missionaries. Willibrord was now Bishop of Utrecht. Political warfare, however, between Duke Radbod and Charles Martel was contrary to Wynfrith's plans for a mission to the heathen. The hopelessness of his situation led to his return to his homeland and to monastic life. In the autumn of 718 Wynfrith left England for Rome.[1] He put himself completely at the disposal of Pope Gregory II as a 'helper of the Church' to work for the Roman Church in Germany and Frisia. He was entrusted with this duty by the Pope and given the name Bonifatius. He travelled through Bavaria to Thuringia.

From Willibald's *Life of St Boniface* (the author was one of his pupils) there is this passage:

> ... so in Thuringia the saint followed out the instructions given to him by the Holy See. He spoke to the elders of the Churches and the princes of the people with words of spiritual exhortation, recalling them to the true way of knowledge and the light of understanding which for the greater part they had lost through the perversity of their teachers.[2]

The Irish and the Celts were the 'bad teachers.' Significantly these were seldom described by the name of their country of origin in the letters of the Pope and Boniface, but rather by the dismissive titles of 'false teachers,' 'seducers,' 'heretics,' and so on. In Thuringia the companions of the Irishman Kilian (died c. 689) had previously carried out missionary work from a centre at Würzburg.

The journey brought Boniface to Frisia once more. He stayed in a number of Celtic monasteries on his way, and this enabled him to acquire a clear idea of the Christianity which was widespread there. He got to know the priests and bishops. It is not known if he had any companions on this first journey. When he arrived in Frisia he called himself by his old name of Wynfrith and avoided using the name of Boniface given him in Rome. He was silent, too, about the papal commission. He was probably silent about this with Willibrord in Utrecht. Willibrord had established an understanding with Rome after a journey there, but in his personal attitude and belief remained completely in the Celtic tradition.[3] In the course of three years he won Willibrord's trust. But when there was consideration of the question of Willbrord's succession and a higher position was proposed for Wynfrith he confessed that as the Pope's representative he could not accept a higher priestly office without Rome's permission. At this Willibrord dismissed him immediately. Ebrard concludes from his research that as well as practical study of missionary work Boniface practised a method of investigation when he was with Willibrord so that as an expert on this region he might the better fulfil his Roman mission later on.

On continuing his travels Boniface had his first success in Germany at the monastery of Amöneburg (Hesse). This monastery was led by twin monks according to Celtic custom. Boniface appeared there purporting to represent Willibrord, who was said to be willing now to support Rome. The brothers at first did not trust him but he succeeded in convincing them, and he gave them baptism according to the Roman rites.[4] With the help of some Benedictines from England he succeeded in carrying out in a very short time a large number of rebaptisms in lower Hesse. These were reported to Rome as 'conversions of thousands of heathen.'[5]

The missionary bishop

In the same year Boniface responded to a request made in a letter from the Pope and undertook a second journey to Rome. There on November 30, 722, as the successful convertor of the heathen and servant of the Church, he was ordained missionary bishop. Willibald reports:

> [The Pope] put into his hands the book in which the most sacred laws and canons of the Church and the decrees of episcopal synods have been

inscribed or compiled, commanding him that henceforth this norm of Church conduct and belief should be kept inviolate and that the people under his jurisdiction should be taught on these lines.[6]

In his oath of office taken by the apostolic grave of Peter, Boniface swore:

> Should it come to my notice that some bishops deviate from the teachings of the Fathers I will have no part or lot with them, but as far as in me lies I will correct them, or, if that is impossible, I will report the matter to the Holy See. And if (while God forbid) I should be led astray into any course of action contrary to this my oath, may I be found guilty at the last judgement and suffer the punishment ...[7]

The next day (December 1, 722) letters of fraternity to Germania were written to ecclesiastical and secular notables. Boniface was to conduct missionary work; in addition, though, 'when he finds those who have been led astray from the path of true faith ... he may reprove them ... But if (which God forbid) any man should attempt to hinder his efforts ... may he be cursed by the judgement of God and condemned to eternal damnation.'[8]

In a letter to Charles Martel, Boniface was introduced and recommended as the 'bishop appointed to the German people.' The secular arm was often called on by his mission, and Boniface visited the court of Charles Martel in person to discuss the papal commission with him.

Despite his various letters of recommendation, Boniface had much to contend with in Thuringia on his second visit there when he tried to work in the spirit of the Pope's letter.

> [He wanted] in his preaching to show them the path of salvation, and he wanted to correct the errors of those whom he found to have digressed in any way from the path of true belief or to have been led into error by the devil's cunning. He wanted to bring them back into the harbour of salvation by his teaching, and instruct them in the Roman doctrine ... [9]

On the Büraburg at Fritzlar there had been a large Celtic settlement with a Brigit chapel. Here Boniface had an ancient centre for worship of the gods destroyed. To his mind ancient worship of the gods was the work of the devil, whereas the Irish were tolerant towards old cults and customs. In a letter to Bishop Daniel of Winchester he complains of the 'false priests and hypocrites' in Thuringia, and that he had to fight them, because they had a hold over the people. He said that there were many who were sinfully married and such people as practised godlessness and lived on milk and honey.[10]

Boniface had once more to turn to the power of Charles Martel, the ruler of the country, for help. Pope Gregory sent a suitable missive to Charles Martel, and the appeal was successful. More and more Celtic clergy were driven away or replaced by Roman clergy. The manifold foundation of monasteries so often attributed to Boniface was for the most part a reorganization of Celtic monasteries. The widespread missionary work of the Celts was seldom mentioned by its original name in the letters by either Boniface or the Pope. Quite understandably from their interpretation of history it seemed never to have existed. And consequently the historical concept has formed that the Celtic Church, which fell under Rome's influence and was transformed, never actually existed.

The archbishop

In February 731 Gregory II died. Boniface immediately established contact with his successor, Gregory III, and in 732 he granted him the pallium to indicate his status of archbishop, and at the same time gave him the right to consecrate or dethrone bishops. Among the written commissions Boniface received from Gregory there is this passage:[11]

> Those whom you say were baptized by Pagans [this means the Celts] and the case is proved should be baptized *again* in the name of the Trinity ...
> You ask for advice on the lawfulness of making offering for the dead. The teaching of the Church is this – that every man should make offerings for those who died as true Christians [that is, Roman Catholics] and that the priest should make a commemoration of them ... But he is not allowed to do so for those who die in a state of sin, even if they were Christians.

Boniface then travelled through Bavaria with a young companion Sturmin. Here there were a number of Celtic bishops and a population which adhered to this form of Christianity. Boniface made plans with the help of Duke Odilo to 'reform Bavaria according to Canon Law.'[12] A certain Gregory of Utrecht had also joined him as a companion, whom Boniface viewed as his successor.

Legate for Germania

Boniface made his third visit to Rome in 737. Gregory III appointed him legate of Germania, and a letter to the bishops of Bavaria introduced Boniface as 'Deputy of the Pope.' He requested them: 'And you should firmly maintain the Church service and the Catholic faith in the manner according to your rules of the Holy Catholic Apostolic Church ... You should reject and obstruct the intrusion of the Britons and false, heretical priests.'[13]

A second missive of Gregory III in 738 went 'to the magnates and people in Thuringia.' It gave instructions that only bishops consecrated by Boniface were to be tolerated. '... and should he by chance find any who have strayed from the true belief or oppose what the dogmas ordain, he is not to be restricted in his actions in any way by you.'[14]

Boniface asserted that in Bavaria 'this people live outside the rule of the Church and have only one [legitimate] bishop.'[15] Consequently a third missive was sent by Gregory to these, for the most part Celtic, bishops in Bavaria and Alemannia. This letter contained no greeting but began with this instruction:

> The Catholic authority orders a synod to be held twice a year, so that canonical security can be investigated. You should therefore organize a synod in Augsburg which should receive Boniface with full honours as the Pope's Deputy and support the command of the Church as the Holy Catholic and Apostolic Church of God, and reject the *heathen rites* and *doctrines* from Britain or from false priest and heretics, ninety-nine in number.[16]

Over his activity in Bavaria the *Vita* of Willibald gives additional information: In Bavaria '... he armed himself with such a holy zeal that he drove out a schismatic who was sunk in heretical delusions, a man by the name of Eremwulf, after first condemning him according to canonical rule .... He renewed the shrine of the true faith ... and drove the destroyers of the Church and corrupters of the people out.'[17] With the agreement of Duke Odilo and the magnates of the country, the new order was established. Boniface had authority to appoint and dismiss bishops, which he used whenever the Celtic bishops did not acknowledge him. Schieffer makes the relevant comment: 'This was a furious clash between the two historical forces ... a standardized institution with general laws and claims to be a universal Church, and a living, justly organized but unregulated ecclesiasticism.'[18]

Pope Zacharias and Boniface

In 741 two supporters of Boniface died: Charles Martel and Pope Gregory III. On the secular side the successors were Pepin the Short and Carloman, the two sons of Charles Martel. Zacharias ascended the See of Peter, a man who understood Boniface's activities completely and who continued to support them. He replied as follows to a letter from Boniface:

> ... many who call themselves priests hardly know what the priesthood is ... As I have said previously, we commend you to suspend them from the performance of priestly duties and the handling of the sacred mysteries. If you

find that they have acted contrary to the laws of the Church in any other matters, consult the canons and decrees of the Fathers and make your decision accordingly.[19]

Duke Odilo does not appear to have been quite convinced by the policy and activity of Boniface. In 744 he appointed the Irishman Virgilius (Fergil). This man spent the years from 741 to 743 at Peppin's court. Peppin had highly esteemed this outstanding Irish scholar.[20] He sent him to Odilo with a recommendation, and Odilo shortly afterwards let him take over the Bishopric of Salzburg with a Roman consecration.

Boniface vigorously attacked Virgilius and called upon Pope Zacharias to help in driving him out. Zacharias answered:

... this Virgilius ... was found guilty by you of deviating from Catholic doctrine ... If it is established that in his opinion there is yet another world and other human beings under the earth [the Irish already had some advanced astronomical understanding], and [there is] another sun and moon, you are to hold a Church assembly and drive him out of the Church after you have stripped him of his priestly status.[21]

He was then to be brought to Rome and condemned, if he was found to be heretical.

In the meantime Virgilius had established himself so strongly in the affections of the people and in the opinion of Duke Odilo that this did not happen. In addition, he had strong supporters in the Celtic bishops of Bavaria and Austria. Virgilius survived Boniface by three decades and remained until his death in 784 a brilliant embodiment of the free, Irish school of thought.

Concilium Germanicum

Carloman was one of the two sons of Charles Martel who at first gave the stronger support to the Romanization plans of Boniface. (Later he chose the Benedictine monastery on Monte Cassino as a refuge and died there.) He had scarcely come to power when Boniface requested him to summon an all-German Council, the *Concilium Germanicum*. This met on April 21, 742 at an unknown place. Only adherents of one school of thought were invited. The Bavarian bishops were not there, and others refused to attend as a protest.[22] Carloman announced: 'In accordance with the advice of the clergy and of my magnates we have appointed bishops in the individual cities and over them have placed Boniface, the emissary of St Peter, as archbishop.'

The additional demand was made by Boniface that in future only bishops consecrated by him should be recognized. The Celtic priests were to be removed from their positions. Celibacy was to be compulsory and Roman vestments were to be the only permitted dress of priests. A special book of laws with punishment clauses was issued:

> We have decided that in accordance with the warning given in the statutes of the Church we shall allow no priest or bishop coming from abroad, no matter from whence he comes, into the service of the Church without the approval of the synod.[23]

In this way a comprehensive device was created for excluding the active exponents of Irish Christianity. A few individual cases are known of the application of these sanctions. One is found in the correspondence of Boniface, as the case was taken as far as a Lateran Council. It concerned Clement of Rouen, 'a Scot':

> Clement attacks the Catholic Church, he denies and rejects the dogmas of the Church of Christ, he condemns the writings and teachings of the Holy Fathers Jerome, Augustine and Gregory ... therefore I also request concerning this heretic that you entrust Duke Carloman with the duty of taking him into custody, so that he can no longer spread this see of Satan.[24]

A fellow-sufferer with Clement of Rouen was Aldebert of Verdun. They both lacked ordination according to Roman rites and were both married. They were both accustomed to assemble the people in the open country by a cross they set up, this being an Irish custom. They were also charged with having built churches without having dedicated them to a saint. In addition they held people back from making a pilgrimage to Rome. In a Council of Soissons they were both dismissed from their office in the presence of twenty-three bishops. In addition Aldebert was anathematized and the crucifixes in the countryside destroyed. An anonymous writer of Mainz reported that 'Aldebert was locked up by Wynfrith [Boniface] in a dark dungeon in the monastery at Fulda, tortured there for a long time, and murdered by the cowherds when he attempted to escape.'[25]

The wave of persecution released by the *Concilium Germanicum* went further. The usual style in which Church history is written, refers to this as follows: 'A fierce conflict developed with the uncanonical elements in the native clergy. But Boniface, after a brief struggle, won. He was able to fight them with the authority of the bishop and drove them out of their churches.'[26]

For Boniface this 'brief struggle' lasted at the outset for twenty years and continued until his death in 754. And the ecclesiastical historian Schieffer maintains accordingly: 'The actual "conversion of the heathen" is only a temporary and territorially limited phase in Boniface's life ...'[27] Apart from the felling of Odin's Oak, nothing is known. He sums up: 'Scholarly attempts to throw light on his "mission-ary methods" have remained without any tangible results.' Ebrard adds that in Boniface's correspondence for over twenty-four years the words 'conversion of the heathen' never occur.[28]

In 747 Carloman visited the monastery of St Gallen. At his command it was obliged immediately to introduce the Benedictine Rule and dress. The monks are said to have continued for some decades to wear the white Irish habit underneath the brown cowl. The beautiful manuscripts of this monastery show a great deal of Irish spirituality survived in St Gallen.

The last years

Already advanced in years, Boniface spent his last years consolidating his work of Romanization. He replaced the Celtic Bishop Milo at Rheims as well as Bishop Gewilib at Mainz.[29] He took over the metropolitan see of Mainz in person. Together with his pupil Sturmin he founded the Benedictine monastery at Fulda. In Cologne and Speyer he established Roman Episcopates. Measures of this sort led again and again to disputes and struggles.

Pepin, until now the major-domo for the Merovingian King Childerich III, had turned more and more to the growing power of Rome. Pope Zacharias rewarded him by helping him to depose King Childerich and placed him in a monastery. Thereupon after the Great Council at Soissons in 751 Pepin was immediately anointed as the new king by the Roman-Frankish bishops. Zacharias died a year later. His successor, Stephen III, visited Pepin personally in 754, and at St Denis near Paris he crowned Pepin again. In return for this Pepin advanced on Italy. He fought against the Lombard king and confirmed the Pope's possession of the Papal States with a deed of gift. At that Pepin was given the title of 'Roman Patrician.' In this way the ever-growing close relationship of the Roman Church with the secular state-power reached a new height. This meant, too, that the suppression of the last refuges of Celtic Christianity in the vast realm of the Carolingians was only a matter of time.

In a letter written by Boniface in his old age to a bishop there is a passage which gives sudden insight into the inner tragedy of the great fanatic: 'From external struggle, from inner fear ... I need counsel and consolation in the anxieties and anguish of my weary spirit.'

Approaching eighty years of age he made his way to the court of Pepin, the king crowned by Rome, in order to discuss with him the state of ecclesiastical affairs in Utrecht and Frisia. Pepin had at Boniface's request appointed his pupil and designated successor Lullus as *praedicator et pastor Germaniae* and Metropolitan of Mainz. Boniface then undertook a campaign against the heathen Saxon.

Boniface spent the winter of 753–754 in Utrecht. He appointed Eoban as the new bishop. In the course of his journey he was set upon by a number of Saxons who killed him and his companions. His body was brought to Fulda, where his veneration as 'Apostle of Germany' was thereafter cultivated. This continues to the present day, contrary to historical reality.

18. A Late Flowering: John Scotus Erigena

In John Scotus Erigena (*c*. 810 – *c*. 877) an Irish scholar enters the light of history, a scholar who acquired his learning in the monasteries of Ireland. At that time, despite the advance of Romanization, there must still have been in a number of these centres an esoteric Christian tendency of the old school and with it a sense of freedom, which Erigena displayed, like all the great Irishmen.

Ludwig Bieler defends the thesis that Erigena learned Greek in Ireland.[1] He appeared in France with other Irish scholars who had been brought over by the French kings. He came to the court school of Charles the Bald in 845, and in 858 was entrusted by the king with the translation from the Greek of the text of Dionysius the Areopagite which had come from Byzantium. It describes the angelic hierarchies in the esotericism of the Eastern Church. The Greek scholar Atanasius, librarian of Pope Nicholas I, wrote a letter to the French king full of praise for Erigena. 'How wonderful it is that this barbarous [!] man from the ends of the earth is master of the words of another far-off language and has such intelligence that he is able to translate it into another language. This has only been brought about by the art of the Holy Ghost.'[2]

Erigena's work on the Greek Fathers of the Church was so thorough that he built a spiritual bridge across Europe, which Pelagius had wanted to build on his travels more than four hundred years earlier. In his major work *De Divisione Naturae* (On the division of nature) he expressed his concept of the central importance of thought. Reason is in his views the helmsman.

> Reason does not fear the danger of the waves and of wrong courses ... Thought is the supreme movement of the soul about the unknown centre or God ... Now we have to follow reason, which traces the truth of things without allowing itself to be restricted by any authority and candidly pronounces and openly describes what it has discovered and researched on its laborious task of painstaking discussion.[3]

'No authority can be allowed to frighten you away from whatever a rational conviction teaches by means of careful study.' He sees humanity and world in five-tiered 'movement,' which in the hierarchies finds its continuation into the cosmos. 'The first type of this movement is found in the objects of nature (minerals), the second in the realm of life constituted by the growth of plants, the third in animals that cannot reason, the fourth exists specifically in humanity and the fifth is found in the nature of angels.'

In Erigena thought develops individual characteristics. We perceive this in the world of belief only a threshold of what in the development of humanity should be replaced by the knowledge which will lead into a deeper stratum of the universal mystery. 'Faith is assuredly nothing other than a starting point, beyond which the knowledge of the Creator begins with a creature possessed of reason.'

Erigena accepted the Apostle Peter as a representative of a titled belief which should find its way forward and should find completion in the Johannine faith: 'You will know the truth, and the truth will make you free' (John 8:32).

John the Evangelist is therefore for him the inspirer of a future Christianity as author of both the Gospel and the Book of Revelation. In an almost forgotten study of the Prologue to the Gospel of John which has been freshly edited in French by Jeanneau only in 1969, he describes these two paths of Christianity.

As a result of his Irish education Erigena was close to the spirit of John. Consequently his writings were considered to be audacious and were soon condemned by the Church. Pope Honorius III as late as 1225 ordered all works of this heretic that still existed to be hunted out and burnt. In contrast to the writings of the Irishman Pelagius his works have nevertheless survived. Here are some extracts from his homily on the Gospel of John:

> O blessed John, not without reason have you been named John, which means in Hebrew: 'to be in harmony with Grace.' For what other pious teacher was called to the task you were called to, that is to penetrate the hidden mysteries and bring their revelation to the doors of thought?
>
> ... Without presumption it can be said that Peter is more the figure of faith and action than of knowledge and deeper contemplation. Believing? Providence gave action and faith to Peter and to John contemplation and knowledge. John rests on the bosom of the Lord, and this illustrates the sacrament of contemplation ...
>
> True contemplation (thoughtful meditation) perceives with penetrating and clear sight the countenance of truth, without being driven back or deceiving itself and obstructed by no cloud ... Both Apostles hurried to the tomb of Christ ... Peter is the first to enter the tomb; he is the symbol of faith, while John stands for intelligence and wisdom. Because faith prepares the way for knowledge, Peter was the first to enter the tomb. 'If you have not faith, you will not know ...' I do not compare the personal worth of these two apostles, but I investigate and glorify the variety of the divine mystery ... Peter is guided by divine revelation; John leads the souls of believers to knowledge of the eternal, living Christ.[4]

Some years before his death Erigena was summoned to Oxford by King Alfred the Great where, according to William of Malmesbury, he was later murdered.[5] Another version claims he died in France. Legend obscures the details of whatever happened. But his spirituality is linked with the Johannine impulse of Celtic Christianity. He lives on in the deeper layers of the Christian West, and he found understanding among the Rosicrucians and the Cathars.

19. Invasions in Early and Later Christian Times

At the beginning of the fifth century Gaul was overwhelmed by Huns, Vandals and West Goths. Many Gallic scholars fled before them to Ireland, saved books and parchments and brought them to safety in the island. It is reasonable to suppose that here a fruitful meeting of Gallic and Old Irish Christianity occurred. As an important result the Irish became familiar with the Greek and Latin classics. It was for Ireland a fertilizing, spiritual invasion which widened the educational store of the Old Irish monasteries. Consequently the development of monastic culture could continue up to the end of the eighth century.

In 795 the Norwegian Vikings appeared on the East Coast, and plundered the island of Lambay, to the north-east of Dublin. At first they were satisfied with raids but they soon appreciated the value of Ireland as winter quarters and a base for their ships. In 832 Thorgilis conquered Armagh, established his quarters there and erected a fortress near the site which later became Dublin. Shortly afterwards the Danes came with the black ships called Dubh-Ghaill, 'black strangers.' There followed fighting on Irish soil between Norwegians and Danes. The Norwegians were the victors and continued with their war of conquest inland against the Irish king. The Island of Saints was turned into an island of war and robber bands, of dreadful devastation, of the destruction of villages, churches and monasteries. Many monks died a violent death.

It is remarkable that the fall of Old Irish Christianity and the onset of Romanization in the eighth century was accompanied by the invasions and occupations of the Norse and the Danes. Just as Gallic monks in the fifth century fled to Ireland from the Continent before the Huns and Vandals, so now hundreds of Irish monks left Ireland, fleeing before the incursions of the invaders to the Continent. Many Irish books and manuscripts were taken across to safety. Ireland, however, lost her monastic libraries and with them almost all the historical sources for its earlier period and its spiritual culture.

A heathen influence entered with the Vikings which changed the function of churches and monasteries. Ota, the wife of the Viking chieftain Turgeis, after 836 proclaimed her oracular sayings on the site of the monastery of Clonmacnoise.[1] Brutalization of manners and naked law of the jungle resulted in a period of destitution and misery throughout the island. It is said that in 1007 the great gospel of Columcille disappeared from the stone church at Kells. Centuries later it was found in a hiding place and is to be found today as the 'Book of Kells' in Trinity College, Dublin. King Brian of Munster (974–1013) who fought successfully against the

Danish and Norse Vikings sent messengers to western Europe to buy back Irish manuscripts. The monastic life was almost completely destroyed and the people estranged from the Church, after suffering two centuries of war, insecurity and plundering. The Roman Church then brought over from the Continent a period of reconstruction which brought about the complete assimilation of Ireland to the Roman religious culture.

Further description of Irish history has no part in this book, although some reference to the tragic and difficult path of the Irish people should not be omitted, a people which still recalls the loss of the treasure of a spiritual past of a high order. The results of invasions, of wars, of plunder and conquest did not make it possible for Ireland to find any rest and prevented her from discovering her own development. Dermot MacMurrogh, king of the province of Leinster, was the first to call for the military help of King Henry II of England when he was fighting to become High King of All Ireland in the twelfth century. This resulted in Henry II erecting his lordship over Ireland in Cashel (County Tipperary), which began the close connection of Ireland with England which had such dire consequences. Between the many counties, baronies and kingships which were held by Normans, Englishmen and Irishmen, there arose endless large and small warlike struggles for power and possession. At time English viceroys were appointed, and for centuries the Irish Parliament was only allowed to meet if the English Crown permitted it.

Henry VIII brought about complete Anglicization in the sixteenth century. When Protestantism brought about the separation of England from Rome, the new organization of the Church in England was carried across to Ireland and led to bitter conflict and persecution. In 1570 Queen Elizabeth was excommunicated by Pope Pius V and the Irish released from their oath of loyalty. A few years later the Pope and the King of Spain financed an invasion by Italians and Spaniards in support of the Roman faith in Ireland. Savage warfare depopulated the country. Irish landed proprietors were expropriated by an evil land-ownership policy. There were countless risings, attempts at liberation, famines, and conflicts which it is impossible to disentangle, and which still flare up uncontrollably in our own time.

Epilogue

How could we ever forget the Island of Ireland,
the source of the radiant dream of such a great light
and where the sun of faith rose for us!

Ermenrich of Reichenau to Abbot Grimald of St Gallen in 860

The task of dealing with the course of historical development in a survey of the phenomena demands abridgement and stringent omissions. This necessarily makes every such description open to justifiable criticism, and the author is usually most conscious of this. On the other hand, this method is free of the danger of drowning in a flood of facts and losing the continuity of the theme. It is right, though, to offer anyone genuinely interested in Old Irish Christianity and Ireland an opportunity to have a synopsis of this development. The expert will find many gaps and possibly come across errors, too. In this connection it must be borne in mind that a lot of contradictory evidence exists in the sources. The author is grateful for criticism in this connection.

Endnotes

Foreword

1 König. 1972, p.25
2 Kühn, H. 1963, 2:9
3 Bieler 1963; Henry 1963; Burckhardt 1964

Chapter 1

1 Steiner [1924] 1973, 13
2 Kühn, H. 1963
3 Lissner 1961, 72f
4 Hülle 1967, 69
5 Röder. 1949, 31
6 Gsänger 1964, 46
7 Ó Ríordáin 1964, 81
8 Jensen 1951, 36
9 Eliade 1964, 492
10 *Ibid*, 411.
11 Kirchner 1955, 45
12 Meyer, A. 1974
13 Borne 1976, 92
14 Ó Ríordáin 1964, 84
15 Schüpbach 1963, 122
16 *Monuments historiques*, No. 13 866
17 Ó Ríordáin 1964, 93.
18 Charpentier 1971, 56
19 Hawkins 1965.
20 Ó Ríordáin 1964, 94
21 Stroth 1787
22 Goethe 1782
23 *National Monuments*, No. 324
24 Steiner [1923] 1982, 72
25 Hartmann 1952, 72f
26 Caesar De Bello Gallico, VI, 14
27 Dottin 1915
28 Stroth 1787
29 Hartmann 1952, 136
30 *Ibid*, 92

Chapter 2

1 Hartmann 1952, 72

2 *Ibid*, 38.
3 Eliade 1964, 52
4 Hartmann 1952, 36f
5 Engler 1962, 93
6 Hermann 1961
7 Kühn, H. 1966
8 *Steirischer Bauernkalender* 1976
9 Kühn, H. 1966, 214
10 Vries 1961, 37
11 Gougaud 1911, 13
12 Ó Ríordáin 1964, Fig. 64
13 Eliade 1964, 275
14 Atkinson 1959, 7
15 Ó Ríordáin 1964, Fig. 65
16 Eogan 1973
17 Ó Ríordáin 1964, Fig. 66/4
18 Hoffman 1940, 124
19 Spahni 1950, 21
20 Irish Antiquities 4
21 Rütimeyer 1920, 5
22 Frick 1943, 34:169
23 Jacot (quoted in Spahni 1950, 13)
24 Ó Ríordáin 1964, Fig. 66/2

Chapter 3

1 Kerényi 1950
2 *Iliad* XVIII, 18.590
3 Layard 1942, 548
4 Edwards 1993
5 Uhland 1866, 3:398
6 Kerényi 1950, 27
7 *National Monuments*, No. 327

Chapter 4

1 Young 2001, 52
2 Rolleston 1911, 82
3 Vries 1960, 86
4 Grosse 1963
5 *De Bello Gallico* VI, 14
6 *De Sito Orbis* III, 2

7 Dillon & Chadwick 1967, 157
8 Reynold 1949, 188
9 Quoted in Moreau 1958, 109
10 Thurneysen 1921, 182f
11 Reynold 1949, 163
12 Dillon & Chadwick 1967, 142
13 Zimmer 1908, 1117
14 Paor & Paor 1958, 25
15 Pokorny 1933, 33
16 Young 2001, 23–26
17 Vries 1961, 225f
18 Noelle 1977, 196
19 Vries 1961, 227
20 Noelle 1977, 198
21 Vries 1961, 229

Chapter 5

1 Bieler 1963, 4
2 Moreau 1958, 106
3 Pokorny 1933, 39
4 Henry 1963, 1:291f
5 Todd 1864, 33ff
6 Delius 1954, 40
7 Bieler 1963, 5
8 Cerebelaud & Cerbelaud 1966, 35
9 Delius 1954, 22
10 *Ibid*, 73
11 Steiner [1923/24] 1977, 100

Chapter 6

1 Vries 1937, 35
2 Macleod 1982, 48
3 Lindholm & Roggenkamp 1969; Kühn, J. 1945, 29; Kutzli 1974, 85
4 Young 2001, 25f
5 Macpherson 1896, 342
6 Eliade 1961, 65
7 Murphy 1961, v

8 Macleod 1982, 74
9 Pokorny 1944, 59
10 Jung & Franz 1971, 269f
11 Young 2001, 223
12 Johann 1953, 193f
13 Atkinson, Robert, 1898, 2:55
14 Macleod 1904, 250 & 248
15 Carmichael 1992, 30
16 *Ibid*, 10
17 *Ibid*, v331
18 *Ibid*, v1
19 *Ibid*, v216
20 *Ibid*, v56
21 Carmichael 1960, 98
22 Carmichael 1992, v201
23 *Ibid*, v82
24 *Ibid*, v311
25 *Ibid*, v259
26 *Ibid*, v77

Chapter 7

1 Delius 1954, 72
2 Meyer 1902, 205
3 Plummer 1925, 103ff
4 Seebass 1883, 20
5 Pokorny 1944, 116f

Chapter 8

1 Delius 1954, 56
2 Henry 1963, 1:167
3 Delius 1954, 49
4 *Ibid*, 48
5 Kenney 1929, 1:275
6 Delius 1954, 80
7 Bieler 1963, 14
8 Kenney 1929, 1:523
9 Cerbelaud & Cerbelaud 1961, 213f
10 Delius 1954, 53
11 Henry 1963, 1:178
12 *Ibid*, 1:69
13 Bieler 1963, 27
14 Gougaud 1911, 320
15 Stokes 1890, 268

Chapter 9

1 Engler 1962, pp. 41, 88, 119

2 Kühn, H. 1963, Fig. 172)
3 Spahni 1950, 27
4 Greith 1867, 164
5 Carmichael 1960, xix
6 Goodspeed 1914, 310
7 Firmicus, sec. 22:1
8 Lemke 1970
9 *Ibid*, 33
10 *Ibid*, 50f
11 Lindholm & Roggenkamp 1969
12 Kühn, J. 1945

Chapter 10

1 Mitford 1972
2 Eliade 1961, 93
3 Tacitus 1948, sec. 39
4 Paor & Paor 1958, 125
5 Voragine 1949, 89
6 Henry 1963, 1:79

Chapter 11

1 Plinval 1947, 55
2 *Ibid*, 52
3 Wiggers 1833, 37
4 Zimmer 1901
5 Bohlin 1957, 20
6 *Ibid*, 13
7 *Ibid*, 25
8 *Ibid*, 25
9 *Ibid*, 37
10 Plinval 1947, 166
11 Wiggers 1833, 100
12 Augustine 1887, c.21; Wiggers 1833, 97
13 Wiggers 1833, pp. 221, 229
14 *Ibid*, 58
15 Jerome 1893, 499
16 Plinval 1947, 55
17 *Ibid*, 55
18 Bohilin 1957
19 Wiggers 1833, 191f
20 Plinval 1947, 101
21 Wiggers 1833, 198f
22 *Ibid*, 205
23 Augustine, Letters 181–183
24 Wigger 1833, 212
25 *Ibid*, 282

26 Cerbelaud & Cerbelaud 1966, 18
27 Steiner [1921] 1969, May 6
28 Goethe 1932, 562f

Chapter 12

1 Eckleben 1885, 12f
2 Stümcke & Klockenbring 1977
3 Delius 1954, 21
4 Patrick 1961, 9, No. 16
5 *Ibid*, 10, No. 20
6 *Ibid*, 11, No. 23
7 *Ibid*, No. 25; 14, No. 33
8 Delius 1954, 27
9 Cerbelaud & Cerbelaud 1966, 35
10 *Ibid*, 17
11 *Ibid*, 40

Chapter 13

1 Cerbelaud & Cerbelaud 1966, 81
2 Stokes 1905, 44
3 Gjerst 1924, 21f
4 Scott 1916, 33f
5 Delius 1954, 20
6 Stokes 1905
7 Adamnan ?1891, 5
8 Bieler 1963, 67
9 Ebrard 1873, 285f
10 Cerbelaud & Cerbelaud 1966, 191ff
11 Bauerreis 1924
12 Kenney 1929, 1:511
13 Hublow 1979
14 Jecker 1927
15 Bieler 1963, 104

Chapter 14

1 Ebrard 1873, 82
2 Laux 1919, 121
3 *Ibid*, 130
4 *Ibid*
5 Oechsli 1926, 2:47
6 Abel 1849, 84
7 Laux 1919, 157
8 *Ibid*, 165

9 Bieler 1963, 90
10 *Anzeiger* 1938, 117f
11 Laux 1919, 230
12 Laux 1919
13 Seebass 1883, 31; Ebrard
   1873, 148f
14 Delius 1954, 67f
15 *Ibid*, 65f; Seebass 1883
16 Laux 1919, 157

Chapter 15

1 Montalembert 1868,
   2:546f
2 Streit 1940; Hartmann, M.
   R. [1946]
3 Cerbelaud & Cerbelaud
   1966, 133f
4 Schieffer 1954

Chapter 16

1 Bieler 1963, 6
2 Cerbelaud & Cerbelaud
   1966, 18
3 Caspar 1933, 2:506
4 Brechter 1941, 5

5 *Ibid*, 235f
6 Schindler 1964, 73
7 Brechter 1941, 256
8 *Ibid*, 258
9 Ebrard 1873, 54
10 *Ibid*, 19f
11 *Ibid*, 47
12 *Ibid*, 60

Chapter 17

1 Buchner 1963 4b:47
2 Talbot 1954, 40
3 Ebrard 1873, 398
4 Wissig 1932, 25
5 Ebrard 1873, 399
6 Talbot 1954, 45
7 *Ibid*, 70f
8 *Ibid*, 71f
9 Wissig 1932, 41
10 Talbot 1954, 116f
11 *Ibid*, 85f
12 Rau 1968, 5
13 Buchner 1963, 4b:129
14 *Ibid*,, 4b:47
15 Schieffer 1954, 183

16 Ebrard 1873, 415
17 Buchner 1963, 4b:501
18 Schieffer 1954, 103
19 Talbot 1954, 103f
20 Cerbelaud & Cerbelaud
   1961, 210f
21 Buchner 1963, 4b:267
22 Schieffer 1954, 208f
23 Buchner 1963, 4b:381
24 *Ibid,* 4b:401
25 Ebrard 1873, 432ff
26 Schieffer 1954, 152
27 *Ibid,* 146
28 Ebrard 1873, 537
29 *Ibid,* 436

Chapter 18

1 Bieler 1952, 218–34
2 Los 1977
3 Noack 1876, 98
4 Jeanneau 1969
5 Los 1977, 91

Chapter 19

1 Delius 1954, 96

Bibliography

Abel, Heinrich Friedrich Otto. 1849. *Die Chronik Frederegars und der Frankenkönige*. Berlin.

Adamnan, St. (?1891). *Life of Saint Columba*. (Trans. D. MacCarthy). Dublin: Duffy.

Anzeiger für schweiz. Altertumskunde. 1936. Zürich.

Atkinson, Richard John Copland. 1959. *Stonehenge and Avebury and Neighbouring Monuments*. London: HMSO.

Atkinson, Robert (editor). 1898. *The Irish liber Hymnorum*. London: Bradshaw.

Augustine, St Aurelius. *De Natura et Gratia*.

— *Epistolae*.

—1887. *Three Anti-Pelagian Treatises of St Augustine*. London.

Bauerreiss, P. Romuald. 1924. *Irische Frühmissionare in Südbayern*. München.

Bellesheim, A. 1890. *Geschichte der kaltholischen kirche in Irland*. Mainz.

Bertrand, Alexandre. 1897. *La religion des Gaulois*. Paris.

Bieler, Ludwig. 1952. 'The Island of Scholars,' *Revue du Moyen Age Latin*, t.8. Strasbourg.

—1963. *Ireland. Harbinger of the Middle Ages*. London: Oxford University Press.

Bohlin, Torgny. 1957. *Die Theologie des Pelagius und ihre Genesis*. Uppsala: Universitets.

Book of Kells. 1974. London: Thames & Hudson.

Borne, Gerhard von dem. 1976. *Der Gral in Europa*. Stuttgart: Urachhaus.

Brechter, Heinrich Suso. 1941. *Die Quellen zur Angelsachsenmission*. Münster.

Brunius, Carl Georg. 1868. *Försök till förklaringar öfver hällristningar*. Lund: Gleerup.

Buchner, R. 1963. 'Briefe des Bonifatius,' *Ausgewählte Quellen zur deutschen Geschichte des Mittelalters*, Vol. 4b. München.

Burckhardt, Titus. 1964. *Von wunderbaren Büchern*. Olten: Urs-Graf.

Caesar, Julius. *De Bello Gallico*.

—1951. *The Conquest of Gaul*. (Trans. Handford). Harmondsworth: Penguin Classics.

Carmichael, Alexander. 1960. *The Sun Dances. Prayers and Blessings from the Gaelic*. Edinburgh: Floris Books.

—1992. *Carmina Gadelica. Hymns & Incantations*. Edinburgh: Floris Books.

Caspar, Erich. 1933. *Geschichte des Papsttums*. Tübingen: Mohr.

Cerbelaud-Salagnac, Georges, and Bernadette Cerbelaud-Salagnac. 1961. *Irlande, Île des Saints*. Paris: Fayard.

—1966. *Ireland, Isle of Saints*. London: Burns & Oates.

Chadwick, Norah Kershaw, *see* Dillon, Myles, and Norah Kershaw Chadwick.

Charpentier, Louis. 1971. *Les Jacques et le mystère de Compostelle*. Paris: Laffont.

Colum, Padraic. 1975. 'Introduction,' *The Complete Grimm's Fairy Tales*. London: Routledge & Kegan Paul.

Coon, Carleton Stevens. 1939. *The Races of Europe*. New York: Macmillan.

Delius, Walter. 1954. *Geschichte der irischen Kirche*. München & Basel: Reinhardt.

Dillon, Myles, and Norah Kershaw Chadwick. 1967. *The Celtic Realms*. London: Weidenfield & Nicolson.

Dottin, Georges, 1915. *L'antiquité celtique*. Paris.

Ebrard, Johannes Heinrich August. 1873. *Die iroschottische Mönchskirche*. Gütersloh.

Eckleben, S. 1885. *Das Fegefeuer des heiligen Patricius*. Halle.

Edwards, Lawrence. 1993. *The Vortex of Life*. Edinburgh: Floris.

Eliade, Mircéa. 1952. *Images et symboles*. Paris: Gallimard.

—1961. *Images and Symbols*. London: Harvill.

—1964. *Shamanism, archaic techniques of ecstacy*. New York: Bollingen, and London: Routledge & Kegan Paul.

—[1951] 1974. *Le chamanism et les techniques archaîques de l'extase*. Paris: Payot.

Engler, Hans Rudolf. 1962. *Die Sonne also Symbol*. Zürich: Helianthus.

Eogan, George. 1973, spring. 'A Decade of Excavations at Knowth,' *Irish University Review*. Dublin.

Firmicus Maternus, Julius. *De errore profanorum religionum*. (French and German translations only).

Franz, Marie Louise von, *see* Jung, Emma, and Marie Louise von Franz.

Frick, E. 1943. *Jahrbuch der schweizerischen Gesellschaft für Urgeschichte*. No. 34. Frauenfeld: Huber.

Gjerset, Knut. 1924. *History of Iceland*. London: Allen & Unwin, and New York: Macmillan.

Goethe, Johann Wolfgang von. 1782. 'Das Göttliche,' ode.

—1814. *Dichtung und Wahrheit*.

—1832. *Faust*.

—1932. *From my own Life. Poetry and Truth*. (Trans. R. O. Moon). London: Alston Rivers.

—1959. *Faust. Part Two*. (Trans. Philip Wayne). Harmondsworth: Penguin Classics.

Goodspeed, Edgar Johnson. 1914. *Die ältesten Apologeten*. Göttingen.

—1950. *The Apostolic Fathers*. New York: Harper.

Gougaud, D. Louis. 1911. *Les Chrétientés Celtiques*. Paris.

—1932. *Christianity in Celtic Lands*. London: Sheed & Ward.

Gregory of Tours. 1927. *The History of the Franks*. (Trans. O. M. Dalton). Oxford: Oxford University Press.

Greith, Care Johann. 1867. *Geschichte der altirischen Kirche*. Freiburg.

Grosse, Rudolf. 1963. *Ein Rätsel keltischer Kunst. Der Silberkessel von Gundestrup*. Dornach: Philosophisch-Anthroposophischer.

Gsänger, Hans. 1964. *Die Externsteine*. Freiburg: Kommenden.

Hartmann, Hans. 1952. *Der Totenkult in Irland*. Heidelburg: Winter.

Hartmann, M. R. [*c*.1946]. *Die Beatushöhlen am Thunersee*. Basel.

Hawkins, Gerald Stanley. 1965. *Stonehenge Decoded*. New York: Doubleday. (Reissued 1970 London: Fontana)

Henry, Françoise. 1963. *L'art Irlandais*. Paris: Weber.

Hermann, Ferdinand. 1961. *Symbolik in der Religion der Naturvölker*. Stuttgart: Hiersmann.

Hoffman, Ed. 1940. *Feste und Bräuche des Schweizervolkes*. Zürich.

Hublow, Karl. 1979. *The Working of Christ in Man. The Thousand-year-old Frescoes in the Church of St George on the Island of Reichenau*. Edinburgh: Floris.

Hülle, Werner. 1967. *Steinmale der Bretagne*. Ludwigsburg.

Irish Antiquities. [n.d.] Dublin: State Office.

Jeanneau, E. 1969. *Homelie sur le prologue de Jean*. Paris: Cerf.

Jecker, Gall. 1927. *Die Heimat des heiligen Pirmin*. Münster.

Jensen, Adolf Ellegard. 1951. *Mythos und Kult bei Naturvölkern*. Wiesbaden.

—1963. *Myth and Cult among Primitive Peoples*. Chicago & London: University of Chicago Press.

Jerome, St. 1893. *Letters and Selected Works*. Oxford: Parker, and New York: Christian Literature.

Johann, A. 1953. *Irland*. Gütersloh.

Jung, Emma, and Marie Louise von Franz. 1960. *Die Gralslegende in psychologischer Sicht*. Zürich & Stuttgart: C. G. Jung Institut.

—1971. *The Grail Legend*. London: Hodder & Stoughton.

Kalevala. The Land of Heroes. 1977. (Trans. W. F. Kirby). London: Everyman.

Keating, J. 1723. *The General History of Ireland*. Dublin.

Kenney, James Francis. 1929. *The Sources for the Early History of Ireland*. New York: Colombia University.

Kerényi, Károly. 1950. *Labyrinth-Studien*. Zürich. Albea Vigiliae.

Kershaw, Norah, *see* Dillon Myles, and Norah Kershaw Chadwick.

Kirchner, Horst. 1955. *Die Menhire in Mitteleuropa und der Menhirgedanke*. Mainz: Akademie der Wissenschaft.

Klockenbring, Gérard, *see* Stümcke, Ida, and Gérard Klockenbring.

König, Marie. 1972. *Am Anfang der Kultur*. Berlin: Gebr. Mann.

Krohn, Herbert. 1963. *Vorgeschichte der Menschheit*. Köln: Du Mont.

—1966. *Wenn Steine reden. Die Sprache der Felsbilder*. Wiesbaden.

Krohn, Kaarle. 1924–28. *Kalewala-Studien*. 6 vols. Helsingfors.

Kühn, Johannes. 1945. *Mythologische Motive in romanischen Kirchen*. Schaffhausen: Columban.

Kutzli, Rudolf. 1974. *Langobardische Kunst*. Stuttgart: Urachhaus.

Laux, Johann Joseph. 1919. *Der heilige Kolumban*. Freiburg: Herder.

Layard, John Willoughby. 1942. *Stone Men of Malekula*. London: Chatto & Windus.

Lemke, Uwe. 1970. *Gotland*. Stuttgart: Urachhaus.

Lindholm, Dan, and Walter Roggenkamp. 1968. *Stabkirchen in Norwegen*. Stuttgart: Freies Geistesleben.

—1969, *Stave Churches in Norway*. London: Steiner.

Lissner, Ivar. 1961. *Rätselhafte Kulturen*. Olten.

—1963. *The Silent Past*. London: Cape.

Löpelmann, Martin. 1944. *Erinn. Alte irische Märchen*. München & Wien: Rohrer.

Los, Cornelius. 1977. *Keltentum — Untergang und Auferstehung. Die altirische Kirche*. Stuttgart: Mellinger.

Macalister, Robert Alexander Stewart. 1937. *The Secret Languages of Ireland*. Cambridge: Cambridge University Press.

Macleod, Fiona [William Sharp]. 1905. *Winged Destiny*. London: Heinemann

—[1910] 1982. *Iona*. Edinburgh: Floris.

Macpherson, James. 1760. *Fragments of Ancient Poetry Collected in the Highlands of Scotland*. Edinburgh.

—1752. *Fingal Reclaimed*. London.

—1896. *The Poems of Ossian*. Edinburgh: Geddes.

Mela Pomponius. *De Situ Orbis*.

Meyer, Albrecht. 1974. *Gavr'inis*. Stuttgart: Freies Geistesleben.

Meyer, Wilhelm (of Spires). 1902. *Älteste irische Liturgie (Turiner Fragment)*. Göttingen.

Mitford, Rupert Leo Scott Bruce. 1972. *The Sutton Hoo Ship-Burial*. London: British Museum.

Montalembert, Charles Forbes Réne de. 1868. *Die Mönche des Abendlandes*. Regensburg.

—1896. *The Monks of the West*. London. Nimmo.

Monuments historiques, No. 13866. Paris.

Moreau, Jacques. 1958. *Die Welt der Kelten*. Stuttgart & Zürich: Kilpper.

Murphy, Gerard. 1956. *Early Irish Lyrics*. Oxford: Clarendon.

—1961. *Early Irish Metrics*. Dublin: Hodges, Figgis.

National Monuments, No. 324 'Kilmogue, Co. Kilkenny.' Dublin.

— No. 327 'Dublin.' Dublin.

Noack, Ludwig. 1876. *Johannes Scotus Erigena*. Berlin: Philosophische Bibliothek.

Noelle, Hermann. 1977. *Die Kelten*. Bergisch Gladbach: Bastei.

Oechsli, Wilhelm. 1926. *Bilder aus der Weltgeschichte*. Winterthur: Hoster.

Ó Ríordáin, Séan Pádraig. 1964. *Antiquities of the Irish Countryside*. London: Methuen.

Paor, Máire de, and Liam de. 1958. *Early Christian Ireland*. London: Thames & Hudson.

Patrick, St. 1961. *Saint Patrick's Writing*. (Trans. Arnold Marsh). Dundalk: Dundalgan.

Plinval, Georges de. 1947. *Essai sur le style et la langue de Pélage*. Fribourg: Université

Plummer, Charles. 1925. *Irish Litanies*. London: Bradshaw.

Pokorny, Julius. 1916. *Irland*. Gotha.

—1933. *A History of Ireland*. London: Longman.

—1944. *Altkeltische Dichtung*. Bern.

Rau, Reinhard. 1968. *Briefe des Bonifatius*. Darmstadt.

Reynold, Gonzague de. 1949. *Les Celtes*. Paris: Universelles de France.

Ríordáin, *see* Ó Ríordáin, Séan Pádraig.

Röder, Josef. 1949. *Pfahl und Menhir*. Neuwied: Jost.

Roggenkamp, Walter, *see* Lindholm, Dan, and Walter Roggenkamp.

Rolleston, Thomas William Hazen. 1911. *Myths and Legends of the Celtic Race*. London: Harrap.

Rühs, Christian Friedrich. 1812. *Die Edda*. Berlin.

Rütimeyer, Leopold. 1920. *Über Schalen — und Gleitsteine im Kanton Wallis*. Basel: Schweizerisches Archiv für Volkskunde.

Schieffer, Theodor. 1954. *Winfried-Bonifatius und die christliche Grundlegung Europas*. Freiburg: Herder.

Schindler, Maria. 1964. *Columban*. Stuttgart: Urachhaus.

Schüpbach, Werner. 1963. Article in *Gegenwart*. Bern: Troxler.

Scott, Archibald Black. 1916. *S. Ninian, Apostles of the Britons and Picts*. London: Nutt.

Seebass, Friedrich Otto. 1883. *Über Columba von Luxeuils Klosterregel und Bussbuch*. Dresden.

Sharp, William, *see* Macleod, Fiona (pseudonym).

Spahni, Jean-Christian. 1950. *Les mégalithes de la Suisse*. Basel: Institut für Ur- und Frühgeschichte der Schweiz.

Squire, Charles. 1912. *Celtic Myth and Legend*. London: Gresham.

Steiner, Rudolf. [1923] 1964. *Initiationswissenschaft und Sternenerkentnis*. (Gesamtausgabe No. 228). Dornach: Steiner.

—[1923] 1968. *Rie Rätsel der Philosophie in ihrer Geschichte als Umriß dargestellt*. (GA No. 18). Dornach: Steiner.

—[1921] 1969. *Die Naturwissenschaft und die Weltgeschichtliche Entwickelung der Menschheit seit dem Alterturm*. (GA No. 325). Dornach. Steiner.

—[1923] 1973. *The Riddles of Philosophy*. New York: Anthroposophic.

—[1923/24] 1977. *World History in the Light of Anthroposophy*. London: Steiner.

—[1923/24] 1980. *Die Weltegeschichte in anthropopsophischer Beleuchtung und als Grundlage der Erkenntis des Menschengeistes*. (GA No. 233). Dornach: Steiner.

—[1923] 1982. *Man in the Past, the Present and the Future, and the Sun-Initiation of the Druid Priest and his Moon Science*, London: Steiner.

Steirischer Bauernkalender. 1976. Graz: Leykam.

Stokes, Whitley. 1890. *Lives of the Saints from the Book of Lismore*. Oxford.

—(Editor). 1905. *Félire Óengusso Céli Dé*. London: Bradshaw.

Streit, Jakob. 1940. *Beatus Legende zur Christianisierung der Schweiz*. Bern.

Stroth, Friedrich Andreas. 1787. *Diodors von Sizilien*. Frankfurt am Main: Bibliothek der Geschichte.

Stümcke, Ida, and Gérard Klockenbring. 1977. *Der Impuls von Lérins*. Stuttgart: Freies Geistesleben.

Tacitus, Publius Cornelius. *Germania*.

—1970. *The Agricola and the Germania*. (Trans. H. Mattingly). Harmondsworth: Penguin Classics.

Talbot, C. H. (Editor). 1954. *The Anglo-Saxon Missionaries in Germany*. London: Sheed & Ward, and New York.

Thurneysen, Rudolf. 1921. *Die irische Helden— und Königsage*. Halle: Niemeyer.

Todd, J. H. 1864. *St Patrick. Apostle of Ireland*. Dublin.

Uhland, Ludwig. 1866. *Gesammelte Schriften*. Vol. 3.

Voragine, Jacobus de. 1948. *The Golden Legend*. New York: Longman.

Vries, Jan Pieter Marie Laurens de. 1937. *Altgermanische Religionsgeschichte*. Berlin & Leipzig.

—1960. *Kelten und Germanen*. Bern & München: Franke.

—1961. *Keltische Religion*. Stuttgart: Kohlhammer.

Wiggers, Gustav Friedrich. 1833. *Versuch einer pragmatischer Darstellung des Augustinismus und Pelagianismus*. Hamburg.

Wissig, Otto. 1932. *Iroschotten und Bonifatius in Deutschland*. Gütersloh: Bertelsmann.

Wotke, Friedrich. 1940. *Das Bekenntnis des heiligen Patrick*. Freiburg.

Young, Ella. 2001. *Celtic Wonder Tales*. Edinburgh: Floris.

—1955. *Keltische Mythologie*. Ahrweiler: Are.

Zimmer, Heinrich, 1901. *Pelagius in Irland*. Berlin.

—1908. *Beiträge zur Erklärung altirischer Texte*. Belin: Preussische Sitzungsberichte.

Index

Figures in *italic* refer to illustrations

Photographic acknowledgements

With thanks to the following for the photographs on the pages indicated:
AKG Images/Eric Lessing 22, The Bridgeman Art Library 105, 120, 172, Des Lavelle 99, 101, Duchas (Photographic Unit, Dept. of the Environment, Dublin) 41, 42, 45, 48 (bottom), 49, 56 (left), 90, 92, 109, 115, 119 (right), 128 (left), 129, 132 (right), 134, 135, 138 (top & middle), 140 (right), 141, 148, 150, 154, Getty Images 21, Jim Dempsey 18, 28, 108, 119 (left), 130, 132 (left), 139, 144, 145, 147, 151, Lars Ims 122, Mary Ann Sullivan 39, 40, Michael Fox at Knowth.com 33, 34, 35, Tom Fourwinds at www.tomfourwinds.com 27, 52, 110, 116, 138 (bottom), Scala Archives 56 (right), Jakob Streit 140 (left).